The Ride Down Mount Morgan

When Lyman Felt skids down Mount Morgan in a Porsche and ends up in hospital with broken bones, both his first wife Theodora and his second wife Leah are summoned to his bedside . . . Betrayal and bigamy, crisis and reconciliation are just some of the themes Arthur Miller probes in his startling new play. In this, his most personal and intimate drama since *After the Fall*, America's greatest living dramatist presents a trio of characters who give voice to a *cri de coeur* as passionate and emotional as any in *Death of a Salesman*.

The Ride Down Mount Morgan received its world première at Wyndham's Theatre, London in October 1991 with Tom Conti as Lyman Felt, Gemma Jones as Theo and Clare Higgins as Leah.

ARTHUR MILLER was born in Manhattan, New York City in 1915. After graduating from the University of Michigan, he began work with the Federal Theatre Project. His many award-winning stage plays include *The Man Who Had All The Luck* (1944); *All My Sons* (1947); *Death of a Salesman* (1949); *An Enemy of the People* (1950), adapted from Ibsen; *The Crucible* (1953), *A Memory of Two Mondays* (1955), and *A View from the Bridge* (presented as a double-bill in 1955); *After the Fall* (1964), *Incident at Vichy* (1964), *The Price* (1968), *The Creation of the World, and Other Business* (1972), *The American Clock* (1980), *The Archbishop's Ceiling* (1977), the double-bills *Danger: Memory!* (1987) and *Two-Way Mirror* (1988) and *The Golden Years*, written in 1940 and first performed on radio in 1987 and on television in 1991. His prose writing includes *Focus*, a novel (1945); *The Misfits*, first published in 1957 as a short story and made into a film and published as a novel in 1961; *Everybody Wins*, a screenplay, published in 1990; a collection of short stories, *I Don't Need You Any More* (1967); and three works of non-fiction, *In Russia* (1969), *Chinese Encounters* (1979), and *'Sales* ... his best-kno ... *A Life* was p ...

Arthur Miller

The Ride Down Mount Morgan

METHUEN DRAMA

A Methuen Modern Play

First published in Great Britain in 1991 simultaneously in hardback and paperback by Methuen Drama, Michelin House, 81 Fulham Road, London SW3 6RB.

Copyright © 1991 by Arthur Miller and Inge Morath Miller as Trustee.

The author has asserted his moral rights.
ISBN 0-413-65700-0 (hardback)
    0-413-65710-8 (paperback)

A CIP catalogue record for this book is available from the British Library.
The front cover photograph is by James Fraser, copyright © Impact Photography.
The back cover photograph of the author is by Gordon Rainsford.
Typeset by Hewer Text Composition Services, Edinburgh.
Printed and bound in Great Britain by Cox & Wyman Ltd, Reading, Berks.

To Inge

The Ride Down Mount Morgan was premièred at Wyndham's Theatre, London on 11 October 1991, with the following cast:

LYMAN FELT	Tom Conti
THEO FELT	Gemma Jones
LEAH FELT	Clare Higgins
BESSIE	Deirdre Strath
FATHER	Harry Landis
NURSE LOGAN	Marsha Hunt
TOM WILSON	Manning Redwood

Directed by Michael Blakemore
Designed by Tanyia McCallin
Music by Barrington Pheloung
Sound by Paul Arditti

ACT ONE

Fleeting chords of music accompany the shifts of time and place.

A hospital bed with LYMAN FELT *in it. In a moment* NURSE LOGAN *enters. She is black. He is deeply asleep, snoring intermittently. His head and torso are covered with bandages, one leg is raised in a cast and one arm at an odd angle. She adjusts the mattress with a turn of a crank, then sits nearby and opens a magazine and idly turns pages, looking at photos. After a moment . . .*

LYMAN (*his eyes still shut*). Thank you, thank you all very much. Please be seated.

> NURSE *turns, looks towards him.*

We have a lot of material . . . not material . . . yes, material . . . to cover this afternoon, so please take your seats and cross your legs. No-no . . . (*Laughs weakly.*) Not cross your legs, just take your seats . . .

NURSE. That was a lot of surgery, Mr Felt. You're supposed to be resting . . . Or you out?

LYMAN (*for a moment he sleeps, snores, then*). Today I'd like you to consider life insurance from a different perspective. I want you to look at the whole economic system as one enormous tit.

NURSE. Well, now! (*Embarrassed laugh.*)

LYMAN. So the job of the individual is to get a good place in line for a suck. Which incidentally gives us the word 'suckcess'. Or . . . or not. (*Snores deeply.*)

NURSE. You keep this up we're going to have to see about another shot . . . (*Goes back to turning pages.*)

> FATHER *enters; wears a Panama hat, carries a cane, smokes a cigarette in a holder, drags a broad black cloth behind him. He comes and bends over* LYMAN *as though to kiss him . . .*

LYMAN *stiffens, utters a cry of mixed fear and hopeful surprise, his eyes still shut.*

FATHER *straightens up and shakes his head mournfully.*

FATHER. Very bad for business.

LYMAN *whimpers pleadingly.*

What you need skates for, you fall down they laugh at you. Never talk business with women, God only makes them for one thing, obey God. Your teeth stick out, ears stick out, everything stickin' out, I'm sorry to say you very stupid boy, big disappointment. (*Shaking his head he moves into darkness.*) Very bad for business.

LYMAN. I promise. Papa! (*Calling.*) I promise! (*He opens his eyes, gradually taking in the* NURSE.) You black?

NURSE. That's what they keep telling me.

LYMAN. You ah . . . RSP?

NURSE. RN? – Yes.

LYMAN. Good for you. I've got a big training programme for you guys, biggest in the industry, and first one to put you in sales. There's no election now, is there? Eisenhower or something?

NURSE. Eisenhower! He's long, long gone. And it's December.

LYMAN. Oh. 'Cause you're more likely to be talking to strangers election time . . . why can't I move, do you mind?

NURSE. You broke some bones. They say you went skiing down that Mount Morgan in a Porsche.

She chuckles. He squints, trying to orient himself.

LYMAN. What's that music? Sounds like Earl Hines.

NURSE. Music? There's no music.

LYMAN (*sings*). 'I'm just breezin' along with the breeze . . .' Listen to that, will you? . . . that just beautiful? (*Whistles the tune for a moment, then falls fast asleep again. Wakes.*) Still have some black friends. Say I'm a nigger underneath. (*Chuckle.*) That's an honour. Jimmy Baldwin liked my stories, when I was still a writer. Long time ago. (*Slight pause.*) My wife used to ski like a Methodist – straight up . . . she used to say I ski'd like an Arab – pants kept falling down. No chairlifts in those days, y'know – used to climb back up the mountain on your skis. Herringbone. Women did it easier 'cause their knees opened wider. Get horny just watching them climb. What'd you say?

NURSE. I didn't.

LYMAN. Oh. And where is this I am?

NURSE. Clearhaven Memorial Hospital.

LYMAN (*it is slowly penetrating*). *Clearhaven?*

NURSE. Your wife and daughter just arrived up from New York.

LYMAN (*canniness attempt, but still confused*) . . . From *New York?* Kinda looking woman, how old?

NURSE. Fifties, probably.

LYMAN (*alarm starts*). Who called them?

NURSE. What do you mean? Why not?

LYMAN. And where is this?

NURSE. Clearhaven. – I'm from Canada myself, I just started here. We've still got railroads in Canada.

LYMAN. Listen . . . I'm not feeling well. What are we talking about Canadian railroads for?

NURSE. No, I just mentioned it as there is a storm.

LYMAN. Now what . . . what . . . what was that about my wife from New York?

NURSE. She's here in the waiting room. And your daughter.

LYMAN (*peering intensely*). – And this is *where?*

NURSE. I told you, Clearhaven Memorial.

LYMAN (*looks around warily*). You have a mirror?

NURSE. Mirror? Sure. (*Takes one out of her purse, goes to him.*) You don't look extra great, I can tell you that now.

LYMAN (*looks at himself, touches bandage in surprise*). Could you . . . touch me? (*She puts finger on his cheek. He lowers the mirror, looks at her, suddenly angry.*) Who the hell called them, for God's sake?

NURSE. I'm new here! I'm sorry if I'm not satisfactory. (*Unnerved, she returns to her chair.*)

LYMAN (*high anxiety*). Who said you're not satisfactory? What's all this unnecessary . . . *verbiage?* – Not verbiage, for Christ's sake, I meant . . . (*Panting.*) Listen, I absolutely can't see anyone and they have to go back to New York right away.

NURSE. But as long as you're awake . . .

LYMAN. Immediately! Get them out of here, okay? (*Stab of pain.*) Oh! – Listen . . . there's nobody else, is there? To see me?

NURSE. Not that I noticed.

LYMAN. Please, quickly, go – I can't see anybody!

Bewildered, she exits.

LYMAN. My God, how could I have done this! – Christ, I can just see them! . . . Oh how terrible! It can't happen, it mustn't happen!

Slipping out from the rear of the cast, he moves into the clear – still in hospital gown, but not bandaged. The empty cast remains on the bed as it was. His eyes wide as he stares at his catastrophic vision . . .

Oh, I can just see it . . . Bessie is weeping, oh poor darling! But not Theo . . . No, Theo is completely controlled, yes . . . controlled and strong . . .

As he speaks the beds move away behind him, and a chintz-covered wicker chair and couch, furniture of the hospital waiting room, truck on. Lights change to brighter, more cheerful tone. His wife, THEODORA and daughter, BESSIE, are seated on the couch.

No-no, it mustn't happen . . . !

He is looking on in high tension, but since he is invisible to the others he may move right up to them, sit beside them, etc.
THEODORA's beaver coat is beside her; BESSIE's cloth coat on her lap. THEODORA is sipping a cup of tea. She is an idealistic, intellectually forceful woman turning fifty now, physically strong, if somewhat stiff and ungainly.
BESSIE, after a moment, is suddenly swept by a fit of sobbing, and covers her face. THEODORA grips her hand.

THEO. Darling, you must try not to.

BESSIE. I can't help it.

THEO. Of course you can. Try to think of all the happiness; think of his laughter; Daddy loves life, he'll fight for it.

LYMAN (*looking on admiringly*). God, what a woman!

BESSIE . . . I guess I've just never had anything really bad happen.

LYMAN. Oh, my dear Bessie . . . !

THEO. But you'll see as you get older – everything ultimately fits together . . . and for the good.

LYMAN (*a mix of love and condescension toward her naivety*). Ah, bless her, what an American!

THEO. – Now come, Bessie. – Remember what a wonderful time we had in Africa? Think of Africa.

BESSIE. What an amazing woman you are, Mother.

NURSE LOGAN *enters*.

NURSE. It'll still be a while before he can see anybody. There's a good motel just up the highway; it's ski season but my husband can probably get you in, he ploughs their driveway.

BESSIE. Do you know if he's out of danger?

NURSE. I think so but I'm sure the doctors will let you know. (*Obviously changing subject.*) I can't believe you made it up from New York in this sleet.

THEO. One does what one has to. – I think I would like to lie down, would you call the motel? It was a terrible drive. . . .

NURSE. Sometimes I feel like going back to Canada – at least we had a railroad.

THEO. We'll have them again; things may take time in this country but in the end we get them done.

NURSE *exits*.

THEO (*turns to* BESSIE, *smiling painfully*). What was so funny?

BESSIE (*touching her mother's hand*). It's nothing . . .

THEO. Well, what was it?

BESSIE. Well, I mean . . . things really don't always get done in this country.

THEO (*disengaging her hand; she is hurt*). I think they do, ultimately. I've lived through changes that were inconceivable thirty years ago. (*Straining to laugh.*) I'm really not *that* naive, Bessie.

BESSIE (*angering*). Well, don't be so upset, it's not important. (*Pause. To heal things . . .*) – They certainly are very nice people around here, aren't they?

THEO. Oh yes. I've often been sorry you never knew small-town life, there *is* a goodness.

BESSIE. I'm wondering if we ought to call Grandma Esther.

THEO. If you like. (*Slight pause.*) She gets so impressively emotional, that's all.

BESSIE. Well I won't if it upsets you.

THEO. Oh, no, I have nothing against her any more; she simply never liked me and I always knew it, that was all. But she loves you.

BESSIE. I know she's a superficial woman, but she can really be so funny and . . .

THEO. Funny, yes.

BESSIE. I've never understood why you feel she's cold.

THEO. I just don't like women who are forever seducing their sons.

LYMAN (*with mock-righteousness*). Right!

THEO. It's a miracle she didn't turn him into a homosexual.

LYMAN. Perfect!

THEO. I used to think it was because he didn't marry a Jew.

BESSIE. But she didn't either.

THEO. What she does never counts, dear. But you go ahead, call her, she is his mother and she adores you.

LEAH *enters. She is about thirty; blondined hair, in an open racoon coat, high heels.* NURSE *enters with her.*

LYMAN (*on the instant she enters, claps hands over his eyes*). No, she mustn't! It can't happen! It mustn't! (*Unable to bear it he starts to flee, but stops as . . .*)

LEAH. After all the money we've put into this hospital it

seems to me I ought to be able to speak to the Chief Nurse, for Christ's sake!

NURSE. I'm doing my best to get her for you . . . !

LEAH. Okay, I'll wait here. (NURSE *starts to go*.) I'm only asking for a little information, dear!

NURSE *exits. Pause.*

LEAH *sits, but quickly stands again and moves restlessly.* THEO *and* BESSIE *observe her indirectly, with polite curiosity. Now their eyes meet. She throws up her hands.*

The same thing when I had my baby here, it was like pulling teeth to get them to tell me if it was a boy or a girl.

BESSIE. Is it an emergency?

LEAH. My husband; he cracked up the car on Mount Morgan. You?

BESSIE. My father. It was a car, too.

LYMAN. Oh dear God, not this way . . . please!

THEO. The roads are impossible.

LEAH. It's that damned Mount Morgan road – there've been half a dozen horrible crashes in the last couple of years . . . I still can't believe it – the man driving on ice . . . and at night yet! It's incomprehensible! (*A sudden explosion.*) Damn them, I have a right to know what's happening! (*She charges out.*)

BESSIE. Poor thing.

THEO. But she *knows* how busy they are . . .

Silence now; THEO *leans back, closing her eyes. Another sobbing fit threatens* BESSIE *who downs it, covers her eyes. Then suddenly she breaks down and weeps.*

Oh, Bessie, dear, try not to . . .

LYMAN (*staring front*). . . . if I could only get myself over to the window . . . and out!

BESSIE (*shaking her head helplessly*). . . . I just love him so!

LEAH returns, more subdued now. She sits tiredly, closes her eyes. Pause. She gets up, goes to a window, looks out.

LEAH. Will you look at that moon? Everybody smashes up in the dark and now you could read a paper out there.

BESSIE. You live around here?

LEAH. Not far. We're on the lake.

BESSIE. It looks like such beautiful country.

LEAH. Oh yes. But I'll take New York any time. (*A great sob bursts from her.*) I'm sorry.

She weeps helplessly into her handkerchief. BESSIE is affected and begins weeping, too.

THEO. Now really . . . ! (*Shakes BESSIE's arm.*) Stop this!

She sees LEAH's indignant look.

You still don't know how serious it is, do you? Why are you carrying on like this?

LEAH (*rather unwillingly*). You're probably right.

THEO (*exulting – to BESSIE as well*). Of course! I mean there's always time to despair, why should . . . ?

LEAH (*sharply*). I *said* you were right, I was agreeing with you!

THEO goes stiff, turns slightly away.

I'm sorry.

Short pause.

LYMAN. What admirable women! What strong, definite characters. Now what would they say next?

BESSIE. You raise things on your place?

LEAH. We grow most of what we eat. We have sixty head of cattle. And we're starting to raise thoroughbreds now, in a small way.

BESSIE. Oh, I'd love that . . .

LEAH. I envy your calmness – both of you. Really, you've made me feel better. What part of New York are you in?

BESSIE. East 74th Street.

LYMAN (*gripping his head*). Oh no! No-no . . . !

LEAH. 74th, really? We often stay at the Carlyle. . . .

BESSIE. Oh, it's very near.

THEO. You sound like a New Yorker.

LEAH. I went to NYU School of Business for three years, and I really love the city, but I was raised here in Elmira and my business is here, so . . . (*She shrugs. Goes to the window again.*)

THEO. What sort of business do you have?

LEAH. Insurance.

LYMAN (*hitting his head*). No! – that's enough, stop it!

BESSIE. Oh, that's what Daddy does!

LYMAN (*hands clasped, facing heaven*). Oh don't, don't let it happen!

LEAH. Well, there's a million of us. You in it, too?

BESSIE. No, I'm at home . . . take care of my husband.

LEAH. I'm hoping to sell out, in maybe three–four years, get a place in New York and just paint morning to night the rest of my life.

BESSIE. Really? – My husband's a painter.

LEAH. Professionally or . . . ?

BESSIE. Oh yes. He's Harold Lamb.

LYMAN. No! – My God!

He rushes out holding his head.

LEAH. Harold Lamb?

LYMAN *returns, unable not to witness this.*

LEAH *has ceased all movement, staring at* BESSIE. *Now she turns to stare at* THEODORA.

THEO. What is it?

LEAH. Your husband is really Harold Lamb?

BESSIE (*very pleased and proud*). You've heard of him?

LEAH (*to* THEO). You're not Mrs Felt, are you?

THEO. Why, yes.

LEAH (*her puzzled look*). Then you . . . (*Breaks off, then . . .*) You're not here for Lyman, are you?

BESSIE. You know Daddy?

LEAH. But . . . (*Turning from one to the other.*) How'd they come to notify *you*?

THEO (*uncomprehending, but beginning to take affront*). What's that?

LEAH. Well . . . after so many years.

THEO. What do you mean?

LEAH. But it's over nine . . .

BESSIE. What is?

LEAH. Your divorce.

THEO *and* BESSIE *are struck dumb. A silence.*

You're Theodora Felt, right?

THEO. Who *are* you?

LEAH. I'm Leah. Leah Felt.

THEO (*a haughtiness begins*). Felt!

LEAH. Lyman is my husband.

THEO. Who *are* you? What are you talking about!

BESSIE (*intensely curious about* LEAH, *she angers at* THEO). Well, don't get so *angry*, for heaven's sake!

THEO. Be quiet!!

LEAH (*seeing* THEO'*s genuineness*). Well, you're divorced, aren't you?

THEO. Divorced! – Who the hell *are* you!

LEAH. I'm Lyman's wife.

THEO *sees she is a serious woman; it silences her.*

BESSIE. When . . . when did you . . . ? I mean . . .

THEO (*in motion again*). She's insane! – She's some kind of a nut!

LEAH (*to* BESSIE). It'll be nine years in September.

THEO. And who performed this . . . this *event*?

LEAH. The Elmira City Hall Clerk, and then a Rabbi the next day. My son's name is Benjamin, for his mother's father, and Alexander for Lyman's father – Benjamin Alexander Felt.

THEO (*with a weak attempt to sustain mockery*). Really!

LEAH. Yes. I'm terribly sorry if you didn't know.

THEO. Didn't know *what*? What are you *talking* about?

LEAH. We have been married over nine years, Mrs Felt.

THEO. Have you! And I suppose you have some document . . . ?

LEAH. I have our marriage certificate, I guess . . .

THEO. You guess!

LEAH (*angrily*). Well I'm sure I do! And I know I have Lyman's will in our safe deposit box . . .

THEO (*helplessly mocking*). And it names you as his wife!

LEAH. And Benjamin his son.

THEO *is halted by her factuality.*

. . . But I guess you have more or less the same . . . is that right?

THEO *is still as a stone.*

There was really no divorce?

BESSIE (*with a glance at her stricken mother . . . softly, almost apologetically*). . . . No.

LEAH. Well, I think we'd better . . . meet, or something. And talk, Mrs Felt? I understand your feelings, but you'll just have to believe it, I guess: – we have a terrible problem. Mrs Felt?

THEO. It's impossible; nine years ago . . . (*To* BESSIE.) that's when we all went to Africa.

BESSIE. Oh, right! – the safari!

THEO (*to* LEAH, *with a victorious, if nearly demented laugh*). We were never closer in our lives! We travelled through Kenya, Nigeria . . . (*As though this clinched everything.*) . . . we even flew to Egypt!

NURSE *enters. It instantly galvanizes all of them. She glances from one to the other.*

NURSE. Doctor Lowry would like to see Mrs Felt now.

For one instant no one moves – then both THEO *and* LEAH *rise simultaneously. This actualization of* LEAH's *claim stiffens* THEO, *forcing her to start assertively toward the* NURSE — *and she sways and starts to fall to the floor.*

LEAH. Catch her!
BESSIE. Mother!

NURSE *and* BESSIE *catch* THEO, *then lower her to the floor.* LEAH *becomes frantic through this collapse, rushing toward the periphery, yelling . . .*

LEAH. Help here, someone's fainted! Where's a doctor, goddamit!

Blackout.

Two upholstered chairs. LEAH *is seated facing* TOM WILSON, *a middle-aged but very fit lawyer who is reading a will, and sipping coffee. After a moment she gets up and moves to a point and stares, eyes filled with fear. Then, dialling a phone, turns to him.*

LEAH. — Sorry I'm not being much of a hostess. Sure you wouldn't like some toast?
TOM (*immersed*). Thanks. I'm just about done here.
LEAH (*dialling*). God, I dread it — my boy'll be home from school any minute . . . (*In phone.*) Put my brother on, Tina. . . . Lou? — I don't know, they won't let me see him yet. What'd Uniroyal say? *What?* Well, call L.A. this minute! I want that business! — But we discussed all this yesterday! Jetlag doesn't last this long. (*Hangs up.*) I don't know what it is; there's no sense of continuity from one day to another any more.

TOM *closes the file.*

I know you're her lawyer, but I'm not really asking advice, am I?

TOM. I can discuss this. (*Returning her the file.*) The will does recognize the boy as his son but you are not his wife.
LEAH (*lifting the file*). But this refers to me as his wife . . .

TOM. That's meaningless – he never divorced. However . . . (*Breaks off, pressing his eyes.*) I'm just stunned, I can't absorb it.

LEAH. I'm still in mid-air some place.

TOM. What'd you ask me? Oh yes – provided the legal wife gets a minimum of one third of the estate he can leave you as much as he likes. So you're very well taken care of. (*Sighs. Leans forward gripping his head.*) He actually flies a plane, you say?

LEAH. Oh yes, soaring planes too. We own one.

TOM. You know, for years he never got off the ground unless it was unavoidable.

LEAH. Oh, he's wonderful in the air. (*Pause.*) I'm not here. I'm simply . . . not here. Can he be insane?

TOM. . . . May I ask you . . . ?

LEAH. Please. . . . Incidentally, have you known him long?

TOM. Sixteen, seventeen years. – When you decided to marry, I assume he told you he'd gotten a divorce . . .

LEAH. Of course. We went to Reno together.

TOM. No kidding! And what happened?

LEAH. God, I'd forgotten all about this . . . (*Breaks off.*) How could I have been so *stupid*! – You see, it was July, a hundred and ten on the street, so he had me stay in the hotel with the baby while he went to the court to pick up his divorce decree . . . (*She goes silent.*)

TOM. Yes?

LEAH (*shaking her head*). It's incredible . . . I was curious to see what a decree looked like . . .

LYMAN *enters, wearing short-sleeved summer shirt.*

no particular reason, but I'd never seen one . . .

LYMAN. I threw it away.

LEAH (*a surprised laugh*). Why?

LYMAN. I don't want to look back. Darling, I feel twenty-five! Come, I have a car and driver downstairs. Are you ready for your wedding? (*Laughs.*) You look stunned!

LEAH (*kisses him lightly*). I never really believed you'd do it, darling.

LYMAN. I wouldn't have believed it either . . .

He sits with her, TOM *a foot or two away.*

There's some primitive connection between us, Leah – your smell, maybe – something that goes down to the depths of my brain. I think of you with another man and I get nauseous.

Pause.

LEAH. I never thought you could commit to a woman.

LYMAN. Maybe I got too old to keep changing beds any more. – But I think it's also that . . . see, I've been very successful, but it was really an accident that I got into business, and it turned out to be a false direction. The only reality to me is still poetry, the words; everything else is smoke blowing away. – I know I'll never write any more – that bird won't sing on a diet of money – but I just can't go on faking emotions. And with you I feel like a rock in the river, you flow around me easy and slow . . . You feel committed, don't you?

LEAH. Yes, absolutely. But can I tell you the wedding vow I wish we could make? – It's going to sound strange, but . . .

LYMAN. No! – Say it!

LEAH. I'm embarrassed but I will; 'Dearly beloved, I promise everything good, but I might have to lie to you sometime'. Could one say that and still love someone? Because it's the truth . . . nobody knows what can happen, right?

LYMAN (*slight pause*). What balls you have to say that! Yes, it's the truth and I love you for it!

He kisses her, then seems distracted.

LEAH. You seem drained – are you sorry you divorced her?

LYMAN. I'm . . . a little scared, that's all, but it's natural. – Tell you what. I'm going to learn to fly a plane . . .

LEAH. But you hate flying!

LYMAN (*lifts her to her feet*). Yes, but no more fear. Ever. Of any kind! – I'm going to fly! Now come to your wedding, Leah, my darling!

LYMAN *exits without lowering his arm. She turns to* TOM.

LEAH. . . . And it was all lies! How is it possible! Why did he do it? What did he want?

TOM. Actually . . . (*Tries to recall.*) . . . You know . . . I think we did have a discussion about a divorce . . .

LEAH. You did? When?

TOM. About nine years ago . . . although at the time I didn't take it all that seriously. He suddenly popped in to my office one day with this 'research' he said he'd done . . .

LYMAN *enters in a business suit.*

LYMAN. . . . I've been looking into bigamy, Tom.

TOM (*laughs, surprised*). Bigamy! – What are you talking about?

LYMAN. There was a piece in the paper a few weeks ago. There's an enormous amount of bigamy in the United States now.

TOM. Oh? But what's the point . . . ?

LYMAN. I've been wondering – how about bigamy insurance? Might call it the Desertion Protection Plan.

TOM (*laughs*). It's a great name for a policy . . . but you're kidding.

LYMAN. I mean this. We could set the premiums very low, like a few cents a week. Be great, especially for minority women.

TOM. Say now! – (*Greatly admiring.*) Where the hell do you get these ideas!

LYMAN. I don't think they're ideas, I just try to put myself in other people's places. (*Laughs, enjoying his immodesty.*) – It's what made me what I am today! Incidentally, how frequently do they prosecute for bigamy any more, you have any idea?

TOM. No. But it's a victimless crime so it can't be often.

LYMAN. That's my impression, too. Get somebody to research it, will you, I want to be sure. – I'll be in Elmira till Friday. (*Starts to leave but dawdles.*)

TOM. Why do I think you're depressed?

LYMAN. Slightly, maybe. (*The self-deprecating grin.*) I'm turning forty-seven this July.

TOM. Fifty's much tougher, I think.

LYMAN. My father died at fifty-seven.

TOM. Well, anyway, you're in better shape than anybody I know.

LYMAN. Famous last words.

TOM. – Something wrong, Lyman?

LYMAN (*slight pause; he decides to tell*). I was having lunch today at the Four Seasons, and just as I'm getting up this woman – beautifully dressed, smile on her face, cool as a cadaver – leans over me and says, 'I hope you drop dead you son of a bitch'. You know what she was talking about.

TOM. I can't believe that's still happening.

LYMAN. Oh, three or four times a year; they don't always come out with it but I can see it in their eyes. But it's okay . . .

TOM. You sure you're not imagining it?

LYMAN. No-no, people still think I turned in my partner to save myself. – Which maybe I did, but I don't think so, I think Raoul paid for his crookedness, period. But I'll always be contemptible to a lot of people, Tom. – I still love that guy, though – we had some great years together building the firm. . . . Well, what the hell, that's life. (*Short pause.*) – This is why you were so against my testimony, isn't it?

TOM. You have a barbed wire conscience, Lyman. I knew how close you were and I thought it would come back to bother you.

LYMAN. I might have lost Theo if I'd gone to jail.

TOM. Well, it's over the dam and out to sea.

LYMAN. I did the right thing; it's just the imputation of

cowardice that . . . (*Breaks off.*) Well, fuck it, I've lived my life and I refuse to be ashamed of it! Talk to you soon. (*Stands, but hesitates to leave.*)

TOM. – Is there something else?

LYMAN. I don't think I have the balls.

A pause. LYMAN *stands perfectly still, controlled; then, facing his challenge, turns rather abruptly to* TOM.

It's funny about you, Tom – I've been a lot closer to other men, but there's nobody I trust like you. (*A grin.*) I guess you know I've cheated on Theodora, don't you?

TOM. Well, I've had my suspicions, yes – ever since I walked in on you humping that Pakistani typist on your desk.

LYMAN (*laughs*). 'Humping'! – I love that Presbyterian jive of yours, haven't heard that in years.

TOM. Quaker.

LYMAN (*confessionally, quietly*). I don't want to be that way any more. It's kind of ridiculous at my age, for one thing. (*With difficulty.*) I think I've fallen in love.

TOM. Oh, don't tell me!

LYMAN (*pointing at him and laughing*). Look at you! – God, you really love Theodora, don't you!

TOM. Of course I do! – You're not thinking of divorce, are you?

LYMAN. I don't know what I'm thinking. It's years since anything like this has happened to me. But I probably won't do anything . . . maybe I just wanted to say it out loud to somebody.

TOM. I have a feeling it'll pass.

LYMAN. I've been waiting for it to, but it keeps getting worse. – I've frankly never believed monogamous guys like you are honestly happy, but with her I can almost see it for myself. And that can't ever be with Theodora. With her I'll be on the run till I croak, and that's the truth.

TOM. You know she loves you deeply. Profoundly, Lyman.

LYMAN. Tom, I love her too, but our neuroses just don't **match**.

TOM. Frankly, I can't imagine you apart from each other – you seem so dependent.

LYMAN. I know. I've always relied on her sense of reality, especially her insights into this country. But I just don't want to cheat any more – it's gotten hateful to me, all deception has. It's become my Nazi, my worst horror – I want to wear my own face on my face every day till I die. Or do you think that kind of honesty is possible?

TOM. I don't have to tell you, the problem is not honesty but how much you hurt others with it.

LYMAN. Right. What about your religion – ? But there's no solution there either, I guess.

TOM. I somehow can't imagine you praying, Lyman.

Short pause.

LYMAN. Is there an answer?

TOM. I don't know, maybe all one can do is hope to end up with the right regrets.

LYMAN (*silent a moment*). You ever cheated, Tom?

TOM. No.

LYMAN. Honest to God? – I've seen you eye the girls around here.

TOM. It's the truth.

LYMAN. Is that the regret you end up with?

TOM *laughs bashfully. Then* LYMAN *joins him. And suddenly, his suffering is on his face.*

. . . Shit, that was cruel, Tom, forgive me, will you? – Dammit, why do I let myself get depressed? It's all pointless guilt, that's all! Here I start from nothing, create forty-two hundred jobs for people and raise over sixty ghetto blacks to office positions when that was not easy to do – I should be proud of myself, son of a bitch! And I am! I am!

He bangs on the desk, then subsides, looks front and downward.

I love your view. That red river of tail-lights gliding down Park Avenue on a winter's night – and all those silky white thighs crossing inside those heated limousines . . . Christ, can there be a sexier vision in the world?

Turning back to TOM.

I keep thinking of my father – how connected he was to his life; couldn't wait to open the store every morning and happily count the olives, rearrange the pickle barrels. People like that knew the main thing. Which is what? What's the main thing, do you know?

TOM *is silent.*

– Look, don't worry, I really can't imagine myself without Theodora, she's a great, great wife! . . . I love that woman! It's always good talking to you, Tom.

Starts to go; halts.

Maybe it's simply that if you try to live according to your real desires, you have to end up looking like a shit. (*He exits.*)

LEAH *covers her face and there is a pause as* TOM *observes her.*

TOM. I'm sorry.

LEAH. He had it all carefully worked out from the very beginning.

TOM. I'd say it was more like . . . a continuous improvisation.

LEAH. What's so bewildering is that he was the one who was pushing to get married, not me . . .

LYMAN *hurries on in a winter overcoat, claps a hand over her mouth.*

LYMAN. Don't tell me it's too late. (*Kisses her.*) Did you do it?

LEAH. I was just walking out the door for the hospital.

LYMAN. Oh, thank God. (*Draws her to a seat, and pulls her down.*) Please, dear, give me one full minute and then you can do as you like.

LEAH. Don't, Lyme, it's impossible. (*Obviously changing the subject – with pain.*) – Listen, up here they're all saying Reagan's just about won it.

LYMAN. Well, he'll probably be good for business. The knuckle heads usually are. – You know if you do this it's going to change it between us.

LEAH. Darling, it comes down to being a single parent and I just don't want that.

LYMAN. I've already named him.

LEAH (*amused, touching his face*). How do you know it's a him?

LYMAN. I'm never wrong, I have a very intimate relationship with ladies' bellies. His name is Benjamin after my mother's father who I loved a lot, and Alexander after my father. (*Grins at his own egoism.*) You can put in a middle name.

LEAH (*an unhappy laugh*). Well, thanks so much! (*Tries to stand up but he holds her.*) He asked me not to be late.

LYMAN. The Russians – this is an ancient custom – before an important parting, they sit for a moment in silence. Give Benjamin this moment.

LEAH. He is not Benjamin, now stop it!

LYMAN. Believe in your feelings, Leah, the rest is nonsense. Reach into yourself; what do you really and truly want? (*Silence for a moment.*) I would drive him to school in the mornings, take him to ball games.

LEAH. Twice a month?

LYMAN. With the new office set up here, I could easily be with you more than half the time.

LEAH. And Theodora?

LYMAN. It's difficult to talk about her.

LEAH. With me, you mean.

LYMAN. I can't lie to myself, darling, she's been a tremendous wife. It would be too unjust.

LEAH. But keeping it secret – where does that leave me? It's hard enough to identify myself as it is. And I can't believe she won't find out sooner or later, and then what?

LYMAN. If I actually have to choose it'll be you. But she

doesn't know a soul in this whole area, it'd be a million to one shot for her ever to find out. I'm practically with you half the time now, and it's been pretty good, hasn't it?

LEAH (*touching her belly*). . . . But what do we tell this . . . ?

LYMAN. . . . Benjamin.

LEAH. Oh stop calling him Benjamin! It's not even three weeks!

LYMAN. That's long enough to be Benjamin – he has a horoscope, stars and planets; he has a *future*!

LEAH. There's something . . . why do I feel we're circling around something? There's something I don't believe here – what is it?

LYMAN. Maybe that I'm this desperate. (*Kisses her belly.*)

LEAH. Are you? – I can't express it . . . there's just something about this baby that doesn't seem . . . I don't know – *inevitable*.

LYMAN. Darling, I haven't wanted anything this much since my twenties, when I was struggling to be a poet and make something of my own that would last.

LEAH. Really.

LYMAN. It's the truth.

LEAH. That's touching, Lyman. . . . I'm very moved.

So it is up in the air for the moment.

But I can't, I won't. It's the story of my life, I always end up with all the responsibility; I'd have to be in total charge of your child and I know I'd resent it finally – and maybe even you as well. You're putting me back to being twelve or thirteen and my parents asking *me* where to go on vacations, or what kind of car to buy or what colour drapes. I hate that position! One of the most sensuous things about you was that I could lie back and let you drive, and now you're putting me behind the wheel again. It's just all wrong.

LYMAN. But when you're thirty-six I'll be sixty.

LEAH. Doesn't mean a thing to me.

LYMAN. Dummy, you're not listening; when you're forty-six I'll be *seventy*.

LEAH. Well it's not eighty. – I've made up my mind, dear.

LYMAN. I thought if we lived together let's say ten years, you'd still be in the prime, and pretty rich, and I'd . . .

LEAH. . . . Walk away into the sunset?

LYMAN. I'm trying to be as cruelly realistic as life, darling. Have you ever loved a man the way you love me?

LEAH. No.

LYMAN. Well? That's the only reality.

LEAH. You can drive me to the hospital, if you like realism so much.

She stands. He does.

You look so sad! You poor man . . .

She kisses him; a silent farewell is in this kiss; she gets her coat and turns to him.

– I won't weaken on this, dear, so make up your mind.

LYMAN. We're going to lose each other if you do this. I feel it.

LEAH. Well, there's a very simple way not to lose me, dear, I guess that's why they invented it. – Come, wait in the hospital if you want to. If not, I'll be back tomorrow. (*She draws him on, but he halts.*)

LYMAN. Will you give me a week to tell her? It's still early for you, isn't it?

LEAH. Tell her what?

LYMAN. . . . That I'm going to marry you.

TOM. I see.

LYMAN *moves into darkness.*

LEAH. I don't understand it; he'd had dozens of women, why did he pick me to be irreplaceable? (*Looks down at her watch, stares in silence.*) God! – how do I tell my boy?

TOM. He's nine now?

LEAH. And worships Lyman. Worships him.

TOM. I'd better get to the hospital. (*He moves to go, halts hesitantly.*) Don't answer this if you'd rather not, but you think you could ever take him back?

LEAH (*thinks for a moment*). How can you possibly ask me that? It's outrageous.

TOM. I'm terribly sorry. I apologize.

LEAH (*curiosity aroused*). – Why? – Would Theodora?

TOM. I've no idea.

LEAH. Why do you ask me?

TOM. I've a feeling it could be important.

LEAH. It's impossible. How could I trust him again? (*Slight pause.*) She struck me as a rather judgemental sort of woman . . . is she?

TOM. Oh, she has a tender side too. – I guess she hasn't had time to think of the future, any more than you have.

LEAH (*slight pause*). – I could never take him back, but all this reminds me of an idea I used to have about him that . . . well, it'll sound mystical and silly . . .

TOM. Please. I'd love to understand him.

LEAH. Well . . . it's that he *wants* so much; like a kid at a fair; a jelly apple here, a cotton candy there, and then a ride on a loop-the-loop . . . and it never lets up in him; and sometimes it almost seemed as though he'd lived once before, another life that was completely deprived, and this time around he mustn't miss a single thing. And that's what's so attractive about him – to women, I mean – Lyman's mind is up your skirt but it's such a rare thing to be wanted like that – indifference is what most men feel now – I mean they have appetite but not hunger – and here is such a splendidly hungry man and it's simply . . . well . . . precious once you're past twenty-five. I tell you the truth, somewhere deep down I think I sensed something about him wasn't on the level, but . . . I guess I must have loved him so much that I . . . (*Breaks off.*) – But I mustn't talk this way; he's unforgiveable! It's the

rottenest thing I've ever heard of! The answer is no,
absolutely not!

TOM (*nods, thinks, then . . .*). Well, I'll be off. I hope it's
not too difficult for you with the little boy.

He exits.

Blackout on LEAH.

LYMAN *is softly snoring; a troubled sleep, however – bad
dreams.*

FATHER *appears, smoker's cough announces him in the
surrounding dimness.*

FATHER. Stay off the roof – very bad for business the way
you fucking all these girls up there. Why you talking so
much to your mother? – she don't know nothing. She
don't want to go Florida with me, she says one state
is enough. Stupid woman. I thought a Jewish woman
gonna be smart. You both a big disappointment to me.
I'm telling you stay off the roof before you make disgrace
for the business.

TOM *enters with* NURSE. *She raises* LYMAN's *eyelid.*
FATHER *disappears, coughing.*

NURSE. He still goes in and out but you can try him.
TOM. Lyman? Can you hear me?

LYMAN *stops snoring but eyes remain shut.*

It's Tom Wilson.

NURSE. Keep going, he shouldn't be staying under this
much by now.

LYMAN (*opens his eyes*). *You* in the store?
TOM. It's the hospital.
LYMAN. Hospital . . . ? Oh Jesus, right, right . . . (*Trying
to focus.*) Give me a second, a little mixed up . . . How'd
you get here?
TOM. Theodora called me.

LYMAN. Theodora?

TOM. Your car is registered in the city so the State Police called her.

LYMAN. I had some weird dream that she and Bessie . . . (*Breaks off.*) They're not here, are they?

NURSE. I told you your wife came . . .

TOM (*to* NURSE). Excuse us, please?

NURSE. But I told him.

She exits.

TOM. They've met, Lyman.

LYMAN. Theo . . . didn't collapse, did she?

TOM. Yes, but she's come around, she'll be all right.

LYMAN. I don't understand it, I think I dreamed the whole thing . . .

TOM. Well, that wouldn't be too difficult, it's all pretty inevitable.

LYMAN. Why're you sounding so brutal?

TOM. There's no time to fool around, you've got things to decide. It's all over television . . .

LYMAN. Oh no, dammit! – Have you met her? – Leah?

TOM. We've had a talk. She's a considerable woman.

LYMAN. Isn't she? – She's furious, too, huh?

TOM. Well, what do you expect?

LYMAN. See . . . I thought I'd somehow divorce Theo later. – But it sort of settled in where I had both of them. And after a while it didn't seem so God-awful . . . What about Bessie? –

TOM. It's hit her pretty bad, I guess.

LYMAN. God, and poor little Benny! Jesus, if I could go through the ceiling and just disappear!

TOM. It's all over the television. I think you ought to issue a press statement to cut the whole thing short. As to your intentions.

LYMAN. What intentions? Just give each of them whatever they want. I'll probably go and live somewhere . . . maybe like Brazil or something . . .

TOM. You won't try to hold onto either of them?

LYMAN. They wouldn't have anything to do with me. My God . . . (*He turns away, tears in his eyes.*) How could I have destroyed everything like this! (*Higher intensity.*) Why did I drive into that storm! – I can't understand it! I had the room in Howard Johnson's, I think I was even in bed . . .

TOM. Maybe it'll clear up. – Can you give Theo a few minutes? She wants to say goodbye.

LYMAN. How can I face her? Ask her to wait till tomorrow, maybe I'll feel a little better and . . .

THEODORA *and* BESSIE *enter;* LYMAN *does not see them as they are above him.*

TOM. They're here, Lyman.

LYMAN *closes his eyes, breathing fast.* BESSIE, *holding* THEODORA *by the elbow, accompanies her to the bedside.*

BESSIE (*whispering in some shock*). Look at his bandages! (*Turning away.*) Oh, Mother!

THEO. Stop that.

Bending to LYMAN.

Lyman?

He can't get himself to speak.

It's Theodora.

LYMAN (*opening his eyes.*) Hi.

THEO. How are you feeling?

LYMAN. Not too bad now. I hope I make sense with all this pain killer . . . Is that you, Bessie?

BESSIE. I'm only here because of Mother.

LYMAN. Oh. Okay. I'm sorry, Bess – I mean that my character's so bad. But I'm proud that you have enough strength to despise me.

BESSIE. But who wouldn't?

LYMAN. Good! – (*His voice starts to break but he controls himself.*) That was well-spoken, Sweety.

BESSIE (*with quick anger*). Don't call me that . . .

THEO (*to* BESSIE). Sshh! (*She has been observing him in silence.*) Lyman? – Is it true?

He closes his eyes.

I have to hear it from you. Did you marry that woman?

Deep snores emerge from the head bandage.

THEO (*more urgently*). Lyman?

BESSIE (*points*). He's not really sleeping!

THEO. Did you have a child with that woman? Lyman? I insist!!

LYMAN *emerges from behind the upstage head of the bed, hands clapped to his ears, while the bandaged figure remains as it was. He is in a hospital gown, but unbandaged.*

Light change; an ethereal colourlessness now, air devoid of pigment.

LYMAN (*agonized cry, ears still covered*). I hear you!

THEO *continues to address the cast's bandaged head, and* BESSIE *is fixed on it as well, but her attitude has become formalized as she too becomes a part of his vision – everything is now super-emphatically threatening to him.*

THEO. What in God's name have you done!

Almost writhing in conflict LYMAN *clears his throat. He remains upstage of the bed.*

BESSIE (*bent over the head of the cast*). Ssh! He's saying something!

LYMAN. I realize . . . how crazy it sounds, Theodora . . . (*Breaks off.*)

THEO. Yes?

LYMAN. . . . I'm not really sure, but . . . I wonder if this crash . . . was maybe to sort of subconsciously . . . get you both to . . . meet one another, finally.

THEO (*with disgust*). Meet *her*?

LYMAN. I know it sounds absurd but . . .

THEO. Absurd! – It's disgusting! She's exactly the type who forgets to wash out her panties.

LYMAN (*wincing; but with a certain pleasurable recognition*). I *knew* you'd say that! – I admit it, though, there *is* a sloppy side to her . . .

THEO. She's the worst generation in our history – screw anybody in pants, then drop their litters like cats, and spout mystic credos on cosmic responsibility, ecology and human rights!

LYMAN. To my dying day I will stand amazed at your ability to speak in complete paragraphs!

THEO. I insist you explain this to me yourself. Lyman? – Lyman!

LEAH *enters*. THEO *reacts instantly*.

There'll be no one in here but the family! (*To* BESSIE.) Get the nurse!

LEAH (*despite* THEO, *she approaches the cast, but with uncertainty about his reaction to her*). Lyman!

THEO (*to* TOM). Get her out of here!

TOM *is immobile, and she goes to him furiously*.

She does not belong here!

LEAH (*to the cast . . . with a certain warmth*). It's me, Lyme. Can you hear me?

THEO (*rushing threateningly toward* LEAH). Get out, get out, get out . . . !

Just as THEO *is about to lay hands on* LEAH, LYMAN *throws his arms up and cries out imploringly*.

LYMAN. I want everybody to lie down!

The three women instantly de-animate as though suddenly falling under the urgency of his control. LYMAN *gestures, without actually touching them, and causes* LEAH *and* THEO *to lie on the bed on which his cast remains.* BESSIE *looks on, motionless.*

LEAH (*as she lies down; voice soft, remote*). What am I going to tell Benny? Oh gee whiz, Lyman, why did you . . . ?

THEO (*lying down beside* LEAH). You have a bitter smell, you should use something.

LEAH. I have, but he likes it.

THEO. Blah. (*To* LYMAN.) And what would you say if one of us took another man to bed and asked you to lie next to him?

LYMAN (*lifting off her glasses*). Oh, I'd kill him, dear; but you're a lady, Theodora; the delicate sculpture of your noble eye, your girlish faith in me and your disillusion; your idealism and your unadmitted greed for wealth; the awkward tenderness of your wooden fingers, your incurably Protestant cooking; your *savoir faire* and your sexual inexperience; your sensible shoes and devoted motherhood, your intolerant former radicalism and stalwart love of country now – your Theodorism! Who can ever take your place!

LEAH (*laughing*). Why am I laughing!!

LYMAN. Because you're a fucking anarchist, my darling! (*He stretches out over both of them.*) Oh what pleasure, what intensity! Your counter currents are like bare live wires! (*Kisses each in turn.*) I'd have no problem defending both of you to the death! Oh the double heat of two blessed wives – this is heaven!

Rests his head on LEAH *while holding* THEO's *hand to his cheek.*

LEAH. Listen, you've got to make up your mind about something.

LYMAN. I'm only delaying as long as possible, let's delay it all till we die! Delay, delay, how delicious, my loving Leah, is delay!

THEO (*sits up*). How you can still go on talking about love is beyond my understanding.

LYMAN. And still I love you, Theodora, although certain parts of your body fill me with *rage*!

THEO. So you simply got yourself some other parts instead.

LEAH, *still lying on her back, raises one leg in the air, and her skirt slides down exposing her thigh.*

LYMAN (*replying to* THEODORA, *kissing* LEAH's *thigh*). That's the truth, yes – at least it was all flesh at first.

LEAH (*stretching out her arms and her body*). Oh how good that was! I'm still pulsing to the tips of my toes. (*Stands, comes up to him.*) You're really healthy, aren't you?

LYMAN (*wry attempt*). You mean for my age? – yes.

LEAH. I did *not* mean that!

He links arms and they walk; the others go dark while bright sunlight hits them.

LYMAN. My health is terrific; in fact, it keeps threatening my dignity.

They sit – as on a park bench.

LEAH. Why!

LYMAN. Well, how do I come to be lounging in a park with a girl, and on a working day! I really hadn't planned to do that this afternoon. Did you know I was going to?

LEAH. No . . . but I never do.

LYMAN. Really? But you seem so organized.

LEAH. In business; but not in pleasure.

LYMAN. What surprised me was the openness of your laughter with those heavy executives at the table.

LEAH. Well, your presentation was so funny. I'd heard you were a real brain, not a comic.

LYMAN. Well, insurance is basically comical, isn't it? – at least pathetic.

LEAH. Why?

LYMAN. You're buying immortality, aren't you? – Reaching up out of the grave to pay the bills, remind people of your love? It's poetry. The soul was once immortal, now we've got an insurance policy.

LEAH. You sound pretty cynical about it.

LYMAN. Not at all – I started as a writer, nobody lusts after the immortal like a writer.

LEAH. How'd you get into insurance?

LYMAN. Pure accident. How'd you?

LEAH. My mother had died, my dad had his stroke, and insurance was something I could do from home. Dad knew a lot of people, being a doctor, so the thing just took off.

LYMAN. Don't take this wrong – but you know what I find terrifically sexy about you?

LEAH. What?

LYMAN. Your financial independence. Horrible, huh?

LEAH. Why? – (*Wryly.*) Whatever helps, helps.

LYMAN. You don't sound married, are you?

LEAH. It's a hell of a time to ask! (*They laugh, come closer.*) I can't see myself getting married . . . not yet anyway. – Incidentally, have you been listening to me?

LYMAN. Yes, but my attention keeps wandering toward a warm and furry place . . .

She laughs, delighted.

It's funny; my generation got married to show its maturity, yours stays single for the same reason.

LEAH. That's good!

LYMAN. How happy I am! (*Sniffs his hands.*) . . . Sitting in Elmira in the sun with you, and your scent still on my hands! God! – all the different ways there are to try to be real!

LEAH. What do you mean by that?

LYMAN. I don't know the connection, but when I turned twenty I sold three poems to the *New Yorker* and a story to *Harper's*, and the first thing I bought was a successful blue suit to impress my father how real I was even though a writer. He ran an appetizer store on 40th Street and Ninth Avenue, Middle Eastern specialties . . . you know, olives, grape leaves . . . all kinds of wonderful-smelling realities. (*Grinning, near laughter.*) And he sees the suit and says, 'How much you pay?' And I said, 'Twenty-nine-fifty,' thinking I'd got a terrific bargain. And he says, 'Pray God keep an eye on you the rest of your life'.

LEAH (*laughs*). That's awful!

LYMAN. No! – It spurred me on. (*Laughs.*) He had two pieces of wisdom – never trust anybody, and never forgive. – Funny, it's like magic, I simply can't trace how we got into that bed.

LEAH (*a glance at her watch*). I really have to get back to the office. – But is Lyman an Albanian name?

LYMAN. Lyman's the judge's name in Wooster, Mass., who gave my father his citizenship. Felt is short for Feltman, my mother's name, because my father's was unpronounceable and they wanted a successful American for a son.

LEAH. Then your mother was Jewish.

LYMAN. And the source of all my conflicts. In the Jewish heart is a lawyer and a judge, in the Albanian a bandit defying the government with a knife.

LEAH. What a surprise you are! –

She stands, and he does.

LYMAN. Being so silly?

LEAH. Being so interesting, and in the insurance business.

LYMAN (*taking her hand*). When was the moment? – I'm just curious.

LEAH. I don't know . . . I guess at the conference table I suddenly thought, 'he's basically talking to me'. But then I figured, this is probably why he's such a great salesman, because everybody he talks to feels loved.

LYMAN. You know? – I've never before with a Jewish girl.

LEAH. Well, you're my first Albanian.

LYMAN. There's something venerable in your eyes. Not old – ancient. Like our people's.

LEAH (*touches his cheek*). Take care, dear.

LYMAN (*as she passes before him to leave he takes her hand*). Why do I feel I know nothing at all about you?

LEAH (*shrugs, smiles*). Maybe you weren't listening . . . which I don't mind if it's in a good cause.

LYMAN (*letting go her hand*). I walk in the valley of your thighs.

She laughs, gives him a quick kiss.

When you move away now, would you turn back to me for a moment?

LEAH (*amused*). Sure, why?

LYMAN (*half-kidding, his romanticism*). I have to take a small commuter plane and if I die I want that vision as I go down –

LEAH (*backing away with a wave*). Bye, Lyman. . . .

LYMAN. Can I ask who that fellow was banging on your apartment door?

LEAH (*caught off-guard*). Somebody I used to go with . . . he was angry, that's all.

LYMAN. Are you afraid of him?

LEAH (*shrugs in an accepted uncertainty*). See you, dear.

She turns and walks a few yards, then halts and turns her head to look back at him over her shoulder.

LYMAN. Beautiful.

She exits.

LYMAN (*alone*). Miraculous. (*Thinks for a moment.*) Still . . . was it really all *that* great? (*A phone is lit up, he goes to it, picks it up, troubled.*) Theo? – Hi, darling, I'm just about to take off. Oh, definitely, it has the makings of a much bigger operation; had a talk with Aetna's chief rep. here, and she's agreed to take us on, so I'll probably be spending more time here. – Yes, a woman; she's got a great agency, I might try to buy into her. – Listen, dear, how about you flying up here and we rent a car and drive through the Cherry Valley – it's all bursting into bloom now! – Oh, I forgot; no-no, you'd better go to your meeting then, it's okay; no, it just suddenly hit me how quickly it's all going by and . . . You ever have the feeling that you never got to really *know* anybody?

She never has; he resents it, and a sharpness enters his voice.

Well, yes, I do feel that sometimes, very much; I feel I'm going to vanish without a trace.

Unhappily now, hidden anger, the romance gone.

Theo, dear, it's nothing against you, I only meant that with all the analysis and the novels and the Freuds we're still as opaque and unknowable as some line of statues in a church wall.

He hangs up. Now light strikes the cast on the bed. He moves to it and looks down at himself. BESSIE, THEO *and* LEAH *are standing motionless around the bed and* TOM *is off to one side, observing.* LYMAN *slowly lifts his arms and raises his face like a supplicant.*

We're all in a cave . . .

The three women now begin to move, ever so slightly at first; their heads turning as they appear to be searching for the sight of something far away or overhead or on the floor.

. . . where we entered to make love or money or fame. It's dark in here, as dark as sleep, and each one moves blindly, searching for another; to touch, hoping to touch and afraid; and hoping, and afraid.

As he speaks the women and TOM *move in criss-crossing, serpentine paths, just missing one another, spreading out further and further across the stage until one by one they disappear.* LYMAN *has moved above the bed where his cast lies.*

Now that we're here . . . what are we going to say?

He bends and enters his cast.

Light change: pigment and the air of the present reality return.

TOM *appears with the* NURSE. *They come to the cast and she examines* LYMAN, *bending close to his face exactly as she did at her first entrance at the beginning of the scene, lifting his eyelid, etc.*

NURSE. He still goes in and out but you can try him. Come, dear, Doctor doesn't want you staying under too long.

TOM. Lyman? Theo wants to come in to say goodbye.

THEO *enters with* BESSIE *and they come to the bed*.

THEO. Lyman? Did you marry that woman? I insist you explain this to me yourself! I insist!

LEAH *enters*. THEO *reacts instantly*.

I'll have no one but the family in this room!

LEAH *proceeds anyway*.

Get out, get out, get out!

As she nears LEAH *to strike her* . . .

An animal outcry from LYMAN's *very bowel. It stops* THEO, *and all turn to look at him as he lies there panting for breath. Now he turns to look at them all.*

LYMAN. My God! – *again?*

THEO (*quietly to* TOM, *mystified*). What did he say?

ACT TWO

The hospital waiting room. TOM *seated with* THEODORA.

TOM. Really, Theo, I wish you'd let Bessie take you back to the city.

THEO. Please stop repeating that! (*Slight pause.*) I need to talk to him . . . I'll never see him again. I can't simply walk away. Is my head trembling?

TOM. A little, maybe. Should you let one of the doctors look at you?

THEO. I'll be all right, my family has a tendency to tremors, I've had it for years when I'm tense. What time is it?

TOM. Give them a few minutes more. – You seem pale.

THEO (*presses fingers against her temples to steady herself*). When you spoke with this woman . . . was there any feeling about . . . what she has in mind?

TOM. She's as much in shock as you. The child was her main concern.

THEO. Really. Somehow I wouldn't have thought so.

TOM. Oh, I think he means everything to her.

THEO (*begrudgingly*). Well, that's nice. – Messes like this are basically comical, aren't they – until you come to the children. I'm very worried about Bessie. She lies there staring at the ceiling. She can hardly talk without starting to weep. He's been her . . . her world. (*She begins to fill up.*) . . . You're right; I think I'll go. It just seemed unfinished, somehow . . . but maybe it's better to leave it this way . . . (*She starts for her bag, stops.*) I don't know what to do. One minute I could kill him, the next I wonder if some . . . aberration got into him . . .

LEAH *enters. They did not expect to see each other. A momentary pause.* LEAH *sits.*

LEAH. Good morning.

TOM. Good morning.

Awkward silence.

LEAH (*asking*). He's not in his room?

THEO (*difficult for her to address* LEAH, *turns to her only slowly*). They're treating his eye.

LEAH. His eye?

TOM. It's nothing serious, he tried to climb out his window during the night. Probably in his sleep. His eyelid was slightly scratched by a rhododendron.

THEO (*a stab at communication*). He must not have realized he's on the ground floor.

Short pause.

LEAH. Hm! That's interesting, because a friend of ours, Ted Colby, called last night – he's commander of the State Police here. They'd put up a wooden barrier across the Mount Morgan road when it got so icy; and he thinks Lyman moved the barrier aside.

TOM. How could they know it was him?

LEAH. There was only one set of tyre tracks in the snow.

THEO. Oh my God.

LEAH. He's worried about him. They're good friends, they go hunting together.

THEO. Lyman hunts?

LEAH. Oh, sure.

THEO *shakes her head incredulously.*

– But I can't imagine him in that kind of depression, can you?

TOM. Actually . . . yes, I think I can.

LEAH. Really. He's always seemed so , . . up with me, and happy.

THEO *glances at her, irked, then away.* LEAH *glances at her watch.*

I just have to settle some business with him for a few minutes. I won't be in your way.

THEO. *My* way? You're free to do anything you like, as far as I'm concerned.

LEAH (*slightly taken aback*). Yes . . . the same with me . . .

in your case. (*Beat.*) – I mean as far as I'm concerned. (*The hostility turns her to look at her wristwatch again.*) I want to tell you . . . I almost feel worse for you, somehow, than for myself.

THEO (*hard laugh*). Why! Do I seem *that* old?

The second rebuff stiffens LEAH.

I shouldn't have said that. I apologize. I'm exhausted.

LEAH (*letting it pass*). How is your daughter? – She still here?

THEO (*a hostile colour despite everything*). In the motel. She's devastated.

TOM. Your boy taking it all right?

LEAH. No, it's wracked him, it's terrible. (*To* THEO). I thought Lyman might have some idea how to deal with him, the kid's always idolized him so. I'm really at my wits' end.

THEO (*bitterly angry, but contained*). We are his dust; we billow up behind his steps and settle again when he passes by. Billie Holliday . . . (*She touches her forehead.*) I can't recall when she died, it's quite a while, isn't it?

TOM. Billie Holliday? Why?

TOM *and* LEAH *observe, puzzled, as* THEO *stares in silence. Then* . . .

LEAH. Why don't I come back in a couple of hours – I've got a nine o'clock conference call and it's getting a bit late . . . (*She stands, goes to* THEO, *and extending her hand.*) Well, if we don't meet again . . .

THEO (*briefly touching her hand, hostility momentarily overcome*). . . . Do you understand this?

LEAH. It's baffling. He's raced the Mount Morgan road, he knows what it's like even in summer.

THEO. Raced? You mean cars?

LEAH. Sure. He has a Lotus and a Z. He had a Ferrari, but he totalled it . . .

THEO *turns and stares at space.*

I was thinking before . . .

THEO. He's always been terrified of speed; he never drives over sixty . . .

LEAH. . . . He reminds me of a frog . . .

THEO. A frog?

LEAH. . . . I mean you never know when you look at a frog whether it's the same one you just saw or a different one. (*To* TOM.) When you talk to him – the television is hounding us; he really has to make a definite statement to stop all this stupid speculation.

THEO. What speculation?

LEAH. You've seen the *Daily News*, haven't you?

THEO. What!

LEAH. We're both on the front page with a headline . . .

TOM (*to* THEO, *placating*). It's unimportant . . .

THEO (*to* LEAH). What's the headline?

LEAH. 'Who Gets Lyman?'

THEO. How dare they!

TOM. Don't be upset, I'll get a statement from him this morning . . .

LEAH. Goodbye, Mrs . . . (*Stops herself; a short laugh.*) I was going to call you Mrs Felt but . . . (*Correcting again.*) Well you are, aren't you – I guess I'm the one who's not! I'll come by about ten or so.

She exits.

THEO. She wants him back, doesn't she?

TOM. Why?

THEO (*a bitter little laugh*). Didn't you hear it? – She's the only one he was happy with!

TOM. Oh, I don't think she meant . . .

THEO (*fiercely*). That's *all* she meant; there's something vulgar about that woman. – I pity her, though – with such a young child. (*She fumes in silence.*) *Can* it have been suicide?

TOM. Frankly, in a way I'd almost hope so.

THEO. . . . It would indicate a moral conscience, is that what you mean?

TOM. Well, I'd hate to think all this duplicity meant nothing to him.

THEO. Unless his mind simply shattered. The Lyman I know could no more hunt animals and drive racing cars than . . .

TOM. I don't know, maybe he just wanted to change his life; do things he'd never done; be a completely different person . . .

THEO (*stares for a moment*). . . . Maybe not so different.

TOM. How do you mean?

THEO (*a long hesitation*). I don't know why I'm still trying to protect him – he tried to kill me once.

TOM. You're not serious.

LYMAN *appears in sunlight in swim trunks, inhaling deeply on a boat deck. She begins walking toward him.*

THEO. Oh yes! I didn't know this woman existed then, but I see now it was just about the time they had either married or were on the verge.

Moving toward LYMAN *her coat slides off, revealing herself in a swimsuit.*

He seemed very strange, unreal. We'd gone for a two-day sail off Montauk . . .

LYMAN *is doing breathing exercises.*

LYMAN. The morning mist rising from the sea is always like the first day of the world . . . the 'oysterygods and the visigods . . .'

THEO *enters into his acting area.*

THEO. *Finnegan's Wake.* Like some tea, dear?

LYMAN. Great! – yes!

Kneels, tuning a radio; static as she pours tea.

I'll get the weather. Is that a new suit? – It's sexy as hell.

THEO. Two years ago. You bought it for me in San Diego.

LYMAN (*mimes pistol to his head*). Bang.

ANNOUNCER (*voice over*). . . . Due to the unusually warm spring tides there've been reported shark sightings off Montauk . . . one is reported to be twelve to fourteen feet long . . .

Heavy static intervenes; he mimes switching radio off.

LYMAN. Jesus.

THEO. Oh, that's ridiculous, it's only May! I'm going in for a dip . . . (*She looks over into the ocean.*)

LYMAN. But the man said . . .

THEO. Nonsense. I've sailed around here since my childhood, and father did and grandfather – there are never sharks till July if at all, the water's much too cold. Come in with me?

LYMAN (*resentfully smiling*). I'm the Mediterranean type – we're unreliable and hate cold water. But go ahead, I'll wait here and admire you.

THEO. Darling, I'm allowed to say that sharks are impossible this time of year, aren't I?

LYMAN (*strained laugh at the outrageousness*). I know I shouldn't say this, Theo, but how you can hang onto your convictions in the face of a report like that . . . just seems . . . I don't know – fanatical.

THEO (*a hard, determined laugh*). Now that is really uncalled for! You're just as stubborn as I am when you're committed to something.

LYMAN. Goddamit, you're right! And I love your convictions! You're just great, honey – (*Swings an arm around her.*) go ahead, I'll keep an eye out.

THEO (*with loving laughter*). You simply can't stand me contradicting you, darling, but it's the best exercise for your character.

LYMAN (*laughs, with her, points front*). Right! And a miserable character it is. Into the ocean! (*He leaves her side, scans ocean.*)

THEO (*bends to dive*). On the mark . . . get set . . .

LYMAN (*points leftward*). What's that out there?

THEO. No, sharks always move, that's a log.

LYMAN. Okay, go ahead, jump in.

THEO. I'll run in! Wait, let me warm up. (*Backs up to make a run for it.*) Join me! – Come on.

LYMAN. I can't, dear, I fear death.

She is behind him, running in place. His back is to her and his eye now catches sight of something toward the right; his mouth drops open, eyes staring in horror following the moving shark. She bends to start her run.

THEO. Okay, one . . . and a two . . . and a . . . three!

She runs and as she comes abreast of him he suddenly reaches out and stops her at the edge.

LYMAN. Stop!

He points front; she looks, horror rising in her face as their eyes follow the fish.

THEO. My God, the *size* of him! Ahhh . . . !

She bursts into tears of released terror; he takes her into his arms.

LYMAN. Honey . . . when are you going to believe something I say!

THEO. Oh, I'm going to be sick . . . !

About to vomit, she bends and rushes into darkness. Light goes out on LYMAN and up on TOM in the waiting room; he is staring ahead, listening. The light widens and finds THEO standing in her fur coat.

TOM. That sounds like he saved you.

THEO. Yes, I've always tried to think of it that way, too, but I have to face everything now – (*Coming downstage; newly distressed by the memory.*) it was not quite the top of his voice. I mean it wasn't . . .

Light flares up on LYMAN in trunks and at top voice and horror, shouts . . .

LYMAN. Stop!!

He stands mesmerized looking at the shark below. Blackout on him.

THEO. . . . It was more like . . .

Light flares up on LYMAN *again, and merely semi-urgently – as he did in the scene.*

LYMAN. Stop.

Blackout LYMAN.

THEO. I tell you he was on the verge of letting me go.

TOM. You're angry now, Theo, I don't think you really believe that. I mean, how could you have gone on living with him?

THEO. Well, we did have two serious breakups and . . . months have gone by without – relations. (*An embarrassed, determined smile as she gradually becomes furious.*) – No, dammit, I'm not going to evade that question. – How I've gone on? Maybe I'm corrupt, Tom. I wasn't, once, but who knows, now? He's rich, isn't he? and vastly respected, and what would I do with myself alone? Why does anybody stay together, once they're realized who they're with? (*Suddenly livid.*) What the hell am I hanging around here for? This is the stupidest thing I've ever done in my life! (*Indignantly grabs her bag.*)

TOM. You love him, Theo. (*Physically stops her.*) Please go home, will you? And give it a few weeks before you decide anything? (*A silence. Then she stifles a sob as he embraces her.*) I know how crazy this sounds, but part of him worships you. I'm sure of it.

THEO (*suddenly screams into his face*). I hate him. *I hate him!*

She is rigid, pale, and he grips her shoulders to steady her. A pause.

– I must lie down. I just have to know what happened, as long as I'm here. We'll probably go back to the City by noon. – Or maybe I'll just leave, I don't know. Call me if he wakes up soon. (*She passes her hand across her brow.*) – I feel I look strange.

TOM. Just tired. Come, I'll find you a cab . . .

THEO. It's only a few blocks, I need the air. (*Starting off, turns back.*) How beautiful the country still is up here – it's kind of surprising that it hasn't been ruined!

She exits.

Alone, TOM *stands staring into space, arms folded, trying to figure an approach.*

Blackout.

LYMAN's *room. He is deeply asleep, snoring placidly at first. Now there is a tensing up, he is groaning in his sleep.* LEAH *and* THEODORA *appear on either side of him, but on elevated platforms, like two stone deities; they are in kitchen aprons, wifely ribbons tying up their hair.*

But something menacing about their deathly stillness as the sepulchral dream-light finds them, motionless in this tableau. After a long moment they animate. As in life they are reserved, each measuring herself against the other.

Notwithstanding the humour of some of their remarks, their manner of speaking is godlike, deathly.

THEO. I wouldn't mind at all if you did some of the cooking, I'm not all that super.

LEAH (*generously*). I hear you make good desserts, though.

THEO. Apple cobbler, yes; gingerbread with whipped cream. (*Gaining confidence.*) And exceptional waffles for breakfast, with real maple syrup, although he's had to cut out the sausages.

LEAH. I can do potato pancakes and szegedina goulash.

THEO (*disapproving*). And all that *paprika*?

LEAH. It has to be blended in, of course.

THEO (*at a loss, sensing a defeat*). Ah, blended in! I'm afraid I couldn't do something like that.

LEAH (*smiling, brutally pressing her advantage*). Oh yes, blended in and blended really *in!* And my gefulte fish is feather-light. (*Clapping her cupped palms together.*) I wet my hands and keep patting it and patting it till it shapes up just perfect!

THEO (*struggling with loss*). He does love my glazed ham. Yes – and my boiled tongue. (*A sudden bright idea.*) Custard!

LEAH (*generously*). You can do all the custard and glazed ham and I'll do all the gefulte fish and goulash . . . *and* the blending in.

THEO. But may I do *some?* Once or twice a month, perhaps?

LEAH. Let's leave it up to him – some months you can do more . . .

THEO. Yes! – and some months you.

LEAH. 'Kay! Would you wash out my pants?

THEO. Certainly. As long as he tells me my lies.

LEAH. Good! Then you'll have your lies and I'll have mine!

LEAH & THEO. Hurrah for the menu!

LEAH (*filled with admiration*). You certainly have class!

LYMAN *chuckles in his sleep as they come together downstage of the cast and embrace each other warmly; and arm in arm walk upstage to his bed. Each kneebends on opposite sides of the bed, resting her chin on the mattress and staring at him from both sides. He changes . . .*

He begins to pant in anxiety, as though imprisoned by their threatening stares. Now each gently but surely grasps one of his hands and sucks on one of his fingers. He writhes in terror, gasping for breath and shouting incoherently. The women stand and go into darkness.

A black cloth bundle, unobtrusive on the floor, stirs and he bends over the edge of the bed and looks down at it. From it a lighter flares, lighting a cigarette; FATHER *sits up and coughs quietly, then inhales the cigarette.*

FATHER. Stupid. Very bad for business.

LYMAN *slips out of the cast, picks up a broad-brimmed Panama hat from the floor and defiantly mimes urinating into it; then with a certain anticipation of violence offers it to* FATHER *who snatches it out of his hands angrily.*

FATHER (*looking into the hat*). What you do here?

LYMAN, *defiance weakening, looks into the hat and becomes intensely embarrassed and grips his crotch. Tries to get behind the bed, but* FATHER *stands and begins to stalk him, the broad black cloth trailing behind him.*

A rhythmic, profound sound as from the centre of the earth.

You piss in your father's hat, you son of a bitch? You Communist, something?

LYMAN. No-no, Pa! – Pumpkin pie!

FATHER. Pumpkin pie? You think you gonna be an American? *You? American?* You make me laugh? (*Looks into his hat.*) How I gonna tip my hat to the customers, full of piss? Very bad for business!

LYMAN (*hopefully enticing*). Fifty thousand dollars?

FATHER. And how you pay me back? More piss? (*Stands with the help of a walking stick, raises the cloth with both hands.*) All you can do? – Piss in your father's hat?! I catch you I show you something. . . !

He tries to throw the black cloth over LYMAN's *head.* LYMAN *skitters away . . .*

LYMAN. Don't, Pa, please. . . !

FATHER (*points with stick at* LYMAN's *penis*). Why everything on you sticks out?

LYMAN *climbs into his cast with little frightened cries,* FATHER *now starts viciously pounding the stick on the bed; with each blow a booming sound resonates as from deep in the earth . . .*

Stay off the roof with those American girls! All whores, these American girls! Very bad for business!

LYMAN *is crying out in terror as the* NURSE *hurries in . . . and* FATHER *disappears into darkness . . . coughing, the black cloth trailing behind him.*

Get off the roof, you got no respect, you stupid?

Underground sound stops. NURSE, *carrying a bowl of water and cloth, heads straight for the cast. She takes his hand, patting it as he whimpers.*

NURSE. All right now, let's come back, come on, dear, come on back . . . (*He stops struggling and opens his eyes.*)

LYMAN. Wah. Oh. What dreams. God, how I'd like to be dead.

NURSE. Don't start feeling sorry for yourself; you know what they say – come down off the cross, they need the wood.

LYMAN. I'm suffocating, can't you open a window?

NURSE. Not any more, I can't.

LYMAN. Huh? – Oh, listen, that's ridiculous, I wasn't trying to climb out, it was just those pills got me crazy . . .

NURSE. Well, maybe later. I got to wash up now. Your lawyer's asking can he come in . . .

LYMAN. I thought he'd gone back to New York. I look terrible?

NURSE (*she swabs his face and hands*). You takin' it too hard. Be different if you deserted those women, but anybody can see how well taken care of they are . . .

LYMAN. Go on, you don't kid me, Hogan – underneath all this cool you know you're shocked as hell.

NURSE. Go on, brush your teeth. (*As he does.*) The last shock I had come off a short in my vacuum cleaner . . . (*He laughs, then groans in pain.*) One thing I *have* been wondering, though.

LYMAN. What've you been wondering?

NURSE. Whatever got into you to actually marry that woman? – Man as smart as you?

LYMAN. Were you talking about ice before?

NURSE. Ice? Oh, you mean . . . ya, we go ice fishing on the lake, me and my husband and my boy. – You're remembering a lot better now.

LYMAN (*staring*). It's going to seem very peculiar – I've never not been married, you know. I have a feeling it's like suddenly your case has been dismissed and you don't have to be in court any more.

NURSE. Don't you talk bad about those women; they don't look mean to me.

LYMAN. I just never felt such jealousy, for one thing, and I've known a lot of women. And she had a fantastic smell; Leah smelled like a ripe, pink, slightly musty cantaloupe. And her smile – when she showed her teeth her clothes seemed to drop off. I don't know, we had some prehistoric kind of connection – I swear, if I was blindfolded and a dozen women walked past me on a sidewalk I could pick out the clack of her heels. I even loved lying in bed listening to the quiet splash of her bath water. And of course slipping into her soft cathedral . . .

NURSE. You have the dirtiest mind I ever seen on an educated man.

LYMAN. I couldn't lose her, Hogan. I couldn't lose her. I could not lose her, and that's why I married her. And those are all good reasons, unless you're married already.

NURSE. I'll get your lawyer, okay?

He seems suddenly overcome, weeps.

Now don't you start that cryin' again . . .

LYMAN. It's just my children . . . you can't imagine how they respected me . . . that's the one thing I just can't deal with . . . (*Bracing himself.*) But nobody's any better, goddamit!

TOM WILSON *enters.*

TOM. May I come in?

LYMAN (*uncertainty, trying to read* TOM). Hi! I thought you'd gone back – something happen?

TOM. Can we talk?

NURSE *exits*.

LYMAN. If you can bear it. (*Grins.*) You despise me, Tom?

TOM. I'm still staggering, I don't know what I think.

LYMAN. Sure you do, but that's okay. (*His charming grin.*) What's up?

TOM. I've been discussing things with the women . . .

LYMAN. I can't bear talking about them – I thought I told you – or did I? – just give them what they want. Within reason, I mean.

TOM. That's the thing – I'm not sure they know what they want.

LYMAN. Go on – they want to kill me, don't they?

TOM. Oh, no doubt about *that*, but . . . I really believe Theo'd like to find a way to forgive you.

LYMAN. Oh no! – that's impossible!

TOM. She's a great spirit, Lyman.

LYMAN. . . . Not that great; I'd have to live on my knees the rest of my life.

TOM. Maybe not – if you were clear about yourselves and came to an understanding . . .

LYMAN. I'm pretty clear now – I'm a selfish son of a bitch. But I have loved the truth.

TOM. And what's the truth?

LYMAN. A man can be faithful to himself or to other people – but not to both. At least not happily. We all know this, but it's immoral to admit it – the first law of life is betrayal; why else did those Rabbis pick Cain and Abel to open the Bible?

TOM. But the Bible doesn't end there, does it?

LYMAN. Jesus Christ? I can't worship self-denial; excuse me, but it's just not true for me. We're all ego, kid, ego plus an occasional prayer.

TOM. Then why'd you bother building one of the most socially responsible companies in America?

LYMAN. The truth? I did that twenty-five years ago, when

I was still trying to deny my unrighteousness. But I don't deny anything any more. – What should I say to them, Tom? What should I do?

TOM. Am I wrong? – You seem deeply depressed.

LYMAN. I dread seeing them again. Especially Bessie. I absolutely can't bear the thought of her . . . Advise me, tell me something.

TOM. Maybe you ought to give up trying to seem so strong.

Slight pause.

LYMAN. What do you want me to say, I'm a loser?

TOM. Well? Right now – aren't you?

LYMAN. Well . . . no, goddamit. A loser has lived somebody else's life, I've lived my own; crappy as it may seem, it's mine. And I'm no worse than anybody else! – Now answer that, and don't kid me.

TOM. All right, I won't kid you; I think you've done these women terrible harm.

LYMAN. You do.

TOM. Theo especially. I think you've raked her soul. If you want to get off this dime you're on I'd begin by confronting that.

LYMAN. I've also given her an interesting life, a terrific daughter, and made her very rich. I mean, exactly what harm are you talking about?

TOM. Lyman, you deceived her . . .

LYMAN (*fury overtaking him*). But she couldn't have had all that if I hadn't deceived her! – you know as well as I that nobody could live with Theo for more than a month without some relief! I've suffered at least as much as she has in this fucking marriage!

TOM (*demurring*). Well . . .

LYMAN. . . . Now listen, you want the rock bottom truth? – I curse the day I ever laid eyes on her and I don't *want* her forgiveness!

TOM. For Pete's sake don't get angry . . .

LYMAN (*instantly caught in his memory*). But your whole picture is just untrue! I ever tell you how we met? – Let's stop talking as though this marriage was made in heaven, for Christ's sake! – I was hitchhiking back from Cornell; nineteen innocent years of age; I'm standing beside the road with my suitcase, and I have to take a leak. So I leave the suitcase and go behind a bush. This minister sees the suitcase and stops, gives me a ride and I end up at an Audubon Society picnic where, lo and behold, I meet his daughter, Theodora. – Had I taken that suitcase with me behind the bush I'd never have met her! – And serious people still go around looking for the moral purpose of the universe.

TOM. Give or take a bad patch or two, you've had the best marriage of anyone I ever met.

LYMAN (*a sigh*). I know. – Look, we're all the same; a man is a fourteen-room house – in the bedroom he's asleep with his intelligent wife, in the living room he's rolling around with some bareass girl, in the library he's paying his taxes, in the yard he's raising tomatoes, and in the cellar he's making a bomb to blow it all up. And nobody's different . . . Except you, maybe. Are you?

TOM. I don't raise tomatoes . . . Listen, the TV is flogging the story and it's humiliating for the women; let's settle on a statement and be done with it. What do you want?

LYMAN. What I always wanted; both of them.

TOM. Be serious . . .

LYMAN. I know those women, and they still love me! It's only what they think they're *supposed* to feel that's confusing them. – Do I sound crazy?

TOM. There's something else we have to discuss . . .

LYMAN. – What's Leah saying . . . anything?

TOM. She's stunned. But frankly, I'm not sure she's out of the question either . . . if that's the move you wanted to make.

LYMAN (*deeply touched*). What size these women have! I wish I was struck dead! (*Weeping threatens again.*) Oh, Tom, I'm lost!

TOM. . . . I'm sorry, but there's one urgent thing. I got a call from Jeff Huddleston at six this morning. He heard it on the radio. He's going to insist you resign from the board.

LYMAN. Not on your life! – I started that company and I'm keeping it! – It's outrageous! – Jeff Huddleston's got a woman stashed in Trump Tower and two in L.A.

TOM. *Huddleston?*

LYMAN. – He offered to loan me one once! Huddleston has more outside ass than a Nevada whorehouse!

TOM. But he doesn't marry them.

LYMAN. Right! – In other words, what I really violated was the law of hypocrisy.

TOM. Unfortunately, that's the one that operates.

LYMAN. Yes. Well not with me, kid – what I wish I do!

BESSIE *and* THEO *enter.* THEO *stands beside his bed staring at him without expression.* BESSIE *doesn't so much as look directly at him. After a long moment* . . .

LYMAN (*downing fear*). My God, Theo – thank you . . . I mean for coming. I didn't expect you . . .

She sits down in a potent silence. BESSIE *remains standing, fiercely aloof. He is openly and awkwardly ashamed* . . .

. . . Hi, Bessie.

BESSIE. I'm here for her sake, she wanted to say something to you. (*Hurrying her along.*) Mother?

But THEO *takes no notice, staring at* LYMAN *with a fixed, unreadable smile. After a long awkward moment* . . .

LYMAN (*to fill the void*). How are you feeling today? I heard you were . . .

THEO (*dead flat; it cuts him off*). I won't be seeing you again, Lyman.

LYMAN. Yes, well . . . I guess there's no use apologizing, you know my character . . . I am sorry, though.

THEO. I can't leave my life lying all over the floor like this.

LYMAN. I'll talk about anything you like, Theo. Make it as tough as you want to.

THEO. I seem confused but I'm not; there's just so much that I . . . that I don't want bottled up in me any more.

LYMAN. Sure, I understand.

THEO. – Do you remember that young English instructor whose wife had walked out on him – and his advice to you about sex?

LYMAN. An English instructor?

THEO. 'Bend it in half,' he said, 'and tie a rubber band around it.'

LYMAN (*laughs, but a little alarmed*). Oh, sure, Jim Donaldson!

THEO. Everyone used to laugh at that.

LYMAN (*her smile is empty, his charm desperate*). Right! 'Bend it in half and . . .' (*Continues a strained chuckling.*)

THEO (*cutting him off*). I *hated* you laughing at that; it showed a vulgar and disgusting side of you. I was ashamed . . . for you and for myself.

LYMAN (*brought up short*). I see. But that's so long ago, Theo . . .

THEO. I nearly ended it right then and there, but I thought I was too inexperienced to make a judgement on something like that. But I was right – you *were* a vulgar, unfeeling man, and you are still.

Anxiously, he glances over to BESSIE *for help or explanation of this weirdness.*

LYMAN. I see. Well, I guess our whole life was a mistake then. (*Angered but attempting charm.*) But I made a good living.

BESSIE. Please, Mother, let's go, he's mocking you, can't you hear it?

LYMAN (*flaring up*). Must I not defend myself? Am I supposed to lie and be destroyed? – Please go ahead, Theo, I'm listening, I understand what you're saying, and it's okay, it's what you feel.

THEO (*seeming perfectly relaxed*). – What was the name of the river, about half an hour's walk past the Chemistry Building?

LYMAN (*puzzled . . . is she mad?*). What river?

THEO. Where we went skinny dipping with those geologists and their girls . . .

LYMAN (*at a loss for a moment, then . . .*). Oh, you mean graduation night. . . !

THEO. . . . The whole crowd swimming naked at the falls . . . and their girls all laughing in the darkness. . . ?

LYMAN (*starting to smile – uncomprehending*). Oh, sure . . . that was a great night!

THEO. I straddled you, and over your shoulder . . . did I dream this? – I recall a white wall of limestone, rising straight out of the river. . . ?

LYMAN. That's right, Devonian. It was full of fossils.

THEO. Yes! Beetle imprints, worm tracks, crustacea fifty million years old going straight up like a white temple wall . . . and we floating around below, like two frogs attached in the darkness . . . our wet eyelashes touching.

LYMAN. Yes.

THEO. It was very beautiful, that evening.

LYMAN. I'm glad you remember it that way.

THEO. You see, I am not at all a Puritan, it is simply a question of taste – that night was inspiring.

LYMAN. Well, I never had taste, we both know that. But I'm not going to lie to you, Theo – taste to me is what's left of life after people can't screw any more.

THEO. You should have told me that thirty years ago.

LYMAN. I didn't know it thirty years ago.

THEO. And do you remember what you said as we floated there?

LYMAN (*hesitates*). Yes.

THEO. No you don't.

LYMAN. I said, 'What could ever come between us?'.

THEO (*immense wonder and relief*). Yes. And did you mean that then? Or was I naive to believe you? Please tell me the truth.

LYMAN (*affected*). Yes, I believed it.

THEO. When did you begin to fool me?

LYMAN. Please don't go on any more . . .

THEO. I am trying to pinpoint when my life died. Just so I can know; that's not unreasonable, is it?

LYMAN. From my heart, Theo – I ask your pardon.

THEO. – When did Billie Holliday die?

LYMAN. Billie Holliday? – oh, I don't know, ten – twelve years ago? Why?

She goes silent, stares into space. He is suddenly on the verge of weeping at the sight of her suffering.

Oh, Theo, I'm so sorry . . . (*She remains staring.*) Why do you want to know about Billie . . . ?

BESSIE. All right, Mother, let's go, huh?

LYMAN. Bessie, I think it might be better if she talked it out . . .

BESSIE. No one is interested in what you think. (*To* THEO.) I want you to come now!

LYMAN. Have mercy on her!

BESSIE. *You* talking mercy!?

LYMAN. For her, not me! – She loved me! Don't you hear what she's trying to say?

BESSIE. How can you listen to this shit!

LYMAN. How dare you! I gave you a damned fine life, Bessie!

BESSIE. You have nothing to say any more, you are a nonsense!

THEO. Please, dear! – Wait outside for a few minutes.

BESSIE, *seeing her adamant, strides out.*

You've torn out her heart.

He turns away trying not to weep.

Was there some pleasure in making a fool of me? What was behind this? Why couldn't you have told me about this woman?

LYMAN. I did try, many times, but . . . I guess it sounds crazy, but . . . I just couldn't bear to lose you.

THEO. But – ! (*Sudden, near-hysterical intensity.*) – You were lying to me every day all these nine or ten years, and before that about other women, weren't you? – what would you possibly lose?

LYMAN (*determined not to flinch*). . . . Your happiness.

THEO. *My* happiness!

LYMAN. I love you.

THEO. You love me.

LYMAN. (*daring to, after a hesitation*). Only the truth can help us, Theo – I think you were happier in these last years than ever in our marriage – you feel that, don't you?

She doesn't contradict.

And I think the reason is that I was never bored being with you.

THEO. You'd been bored with me?

LYMAN. Same as you'd been with me, dear . . . I'm talking about – you know – just normal marital boredom.

But she seems obtuse to this, so he tries to explain.

You know, like at dinner – when I'd repeat some story you'd heard a thousand times . . . ? Like my grandfather losing three fingers under the Ninth Avenue trolley . . . ?

THEO. But I loved that story! I was *never* bored with you . . . stupid as that was.

LYMAN (*now she just seems perverse*). Theo, you were bored – it's no sin! Same as I was when you'd start telling people for the ten thousandth time that – for instance . . . (*His charming laugh.*) as a minister's daughter you were not permitted to climb a tree and show off your panties?

THEO (*sternly resisting his charm*). But I think people are interested in a kind of society that has completely disappeared! That story has historical importance!

LYMAN (*the full agony*). But darling, that story is engraved in my flesh! . . . And I beg you, don't make this a moral dilemma, it's simply a question of reading the same page of a newspaper for thirty years! It is just common ordinary domestic tedium, dear, it is life, and there's no other woman I know who has the honesty and strength to accept it as life – if you wanted to!

THEO (*a pause; above her confusion, she is striving desperately to understand*). And why do you say I was happier in these last years?

LYMAN. Because you could see my contentment, and I was content . . .

THEO. Because she . . . ?

LYMAN. Because whenever you started with your panties again I could still find you lovable, knowing that the story was not going to be my entire fate till the day I died.

THEO. . . . Because she was waiting for you.

LYMAN. Right.

THEO. You were never bored with *her*?

LYMAN. Oh God yes! Sometimes even more than with you.

THEO (*quick intense hopeful curiosity*). Really! And what then?

LYMAN. Then I would thank my luck that I had you to come back to. – I know how hard this is to understand, Theo.

THEO. No-no . . . I guess I've always known it.

LYMAN. What?

THEO. You are some kind of . . . of giant clam.

LYMAN. Clam?

THEO. Waiting on the bottom for whatever happens to fall from the ocean into your mouth; you are simply a craving, and that craving you call love. You are a kind of monster, and I think you even know it, don't you? I can almost begin to pity you, Lyman. (*She turns to leave.*) I hope you make a good recovery. It's all very clear now, I'm glad I stayed.

LYMAN. It's amazing – the minute the mystery of life appears, you think everything's cleared up.

THEO. There's no mystery to me, you have never loved anyone!

LYMAN. Then explain to yourself how this worthless, loveless, treacherous clam, could have single-handedly made two such different women happier than they'd ever been in their lives!

THEO. Really! (*Laughs ending in a near-scream.*) Really and truly *happy*?!

LYMAN (*stepping out of the cast, outraged* – THEO *remaining fixed on the cast*). . . . In fact, if I dared admit the whole idiotic truth, the only one who suffered these past nine years – was *me*!

An enormous echoing roar fills the theatre – the roar of a lion.

Light rises on BESSIE *looking front through field glasses; she is wearing shorts and pith helmet and khaki safari jacket.*

THEO. *You suffering?* – oh dear God save us!

She is trying to sustain her bitter laughing and moves toward BESSIE, *and as she enters the area her laughter dies off and she takes a pith helmet out of a picnic basket and puts it on.*

LYMAN *follows* THEO. *There is no dialogue break.*

LYMAN. . . . What would you call it, then – having to look into your innocent, contented faces, when I knew the hollowness your happiness was based on? That isn't suffering?

He takes his place beside the two women, looking in the same direction out front, shading his eyes. With no break in dialogue . . .

BESSIE (*looking through field glasses*). Good heavens, is he going to mount her *again*?

LYMAN. They don't call him King of the Beasts for nothing, honey.

BESSIE. Poor thing, how patient she is.

THEO (*taking the glasses from her*). Oh come, dear, she's not *only* patient.

BESSIE (*spreading a table cloth on the ground and picnic things*). But it's only once every half a year, isn't it?

LYMAN. Once that we *know* about.

THEO (*helping spread the picnic*). Oh no, they're marvellously loyal couples.

LYMAN. No, dear, they have harems; you're thinking of storks.

BESSIE (*offering an egg*). Daddy?

LYMAN (*sitting – happily eating*). I love you in those helmets, you look like two noble ladies on safari.

THEO (*stretching out on the ground*). The air here! The silence. These hills.

BESSIE. Thanks for bringing me, Daddy. I'm so sorry Harold had to do those lectures. I'll never forget this trip. – Why do you look sad?

LYMAN. Me? No.

THEO. It's just guilt.

LYMAN (*alarmed*). Guilt?

THEO. He's been away from the office for a whole week.

LYMAN (*relieved*). Oh. Actually, why do we think of monogamy as a higher form of life?

THEO. Well, it implies an intensification of love.

LYMAN. How about that, Bess? You had a lot of boyfriends before Harold, didn't you?

BESSIE. Well . . . yes, I guess it is more intense with one.

LYMAN. But how does that make it a higher form?

THEO. Monogamy strengthens the family; random screwing undermines it.

LYMAN. But as one neurotic to another, what's so good about strengthening the family?

THEO. Well, for one thing it enhances liberty.

BESSIE (*puzzled*). Liberty? Really?

THEO. The family disciplines its members; when the family is weak the state has to move in; so the stronger the family the fewer the police. And that is why monogamy is a higher form.

LYMAN. Jesus, did you just make that up? (*To* BESSIE.) Isn't she marvellous? I'm giving her an A-plus!

THEO (*happily hurt*). Oh shut up.

LYMAN. But what about the Muslims? They're very big

on stable families but a lot of them have two or three wives.

THEO. But only one is really the *wife*.

LYMAN. Not according to my father – they often had two main women, one to run the house and one for the bed. But they were both serious wives.

THEO. Your father's sociology was on a par with his morals – non-existent.

LYMAN (*laughs; to* BESSIE). Your mother is a classical woman, you know why?

BESSIE (*laughing delightedly*). Why?

LYMAN. Because she is always clear and consistent and . . .

THEO. . . . Rather boring.

He guffaws warmly, clapping his hands over his head in appreciation.

BESSIE. You are not boring! (*Rushing to embrace* THEO.) Tell her she is not boring!

LYMAN (*embracing* THEO *with* BESSIE). Please no . . . I swear I didn't mean boring!

THEO (*tearfully hurt*). Well I'd rather be boring and clear than cute and stupid!

BESSIE. But I don't think he meant . . .

LYMAN. Who asked you to be cute?

THEO (*a tortured look*). I wish I knew how to amuse you!

LYMAN. I swear to God I am not bored, Theo! – Now please don't go on about it!

THEO. Your eyes have been glazed over since we stepped onto this wretched continent!

LYMAN (*guiltily stretching an awkward embrace toward her*). I *love* this trip, and being with both of you. . . ! Theo, please! – Now you are making me guilty!

The lion's roar interrupts and they all look front in shock.

BESSIE. Is he heading here. . . ? Daddy! – He's trotting!

GUIDE'S VOICE (*off on bullhorn*). You will have to come back to the car, everyone! At once!

LYMAN. Quick!

He pushes both women off.

BESSIE (*on exiting*). Daddy, come. . . !
THEO (*sensing he is remaining behind*). Lyman. . . ?
LYMAN. Go!

He pushes her off, but turns back himself.

GUIDE'S VOICE. Come back to the car at once, Mr Felt!

Lion's roar – but closer now. LYMAN *facing front and the lion, prepared to run for it but holding his ground.*

Mr Felt, get back to the car!

Another roar!

LYMAN (*eyes on the 'lion', shouting toward it with fear's exhilaration*). I *am* happy, yes! That I'm married to Theodora and have Bessie . . . yes, *and Leah, too*!

Another roar!

BESSIE (*from a distance*). Daddy, please come here!
LYMAN. And that I've made a mountain of money . . . yes, and have no pending lawsuits! –
BESSIE (*from a distance*). Daddy. . . !
LYMAN (*flinging his words toward the approaching beast, but crouched and ready to flee*). . . . And that I don't sacrifice one precious day to things I don't believe in – and that includes monogamy, yes, we love our lives, you goddam lion!

Wide-eyed, still crouched to run, he is watching the approaching lion – whose roar, as we now hear, has changed to a rather more relaxed guttural growling, much diminished; and LYMAN *cautiously straightens up, and turns triumphantly toward the women offstage. And* BESSIE *flies out and throws her arms around him in ecstatic relief, kissing him.*

BESSIE (*looking front*). Daddy, he turned back! What did you do that for!

THEO *enters.*

THEO. He turned back! (*To him.*) How did you do that! (*To* BESSIE.) Did you see how he stopped and looked at him and turned around? (*To* LYMAN.) What happened?

LYMAN. I think . . . he sensed that I – darling, I think I've lost my guilt!

THEO. What!

LYMAN (*staring in wonder*). His roar hit my teeth like voltage and suddenly, it was so clear that . . . (*Turns to her.*) I've always been happy with you, Theo! – I'm a happy man and I am never going to apologize for it again!

THEO (*tears of gratitude, clasping her hands together prayerfully*). Oh, Lyman! (*Rushing to kiss him.*) Oh, darling!

LYMAN (*still riding his wave, holding out his hand to her*). What old good friends we are, Theo! Put her there! (*She laughs and manfully shakes hands.*) What a *person* you are, what a grave and beautiful face you have!

BESSIE. Oh, Daddy, that's so lovely! – You're just *marvellous*! (*She weeps.*)

LYMAN. How the hell are we still together – do you realize how she must love me to stand for my character? Well I love her too! I definitely worship this woman, Bessie!

THEO. Oh, this is what I always saw happening some day! (*A sophisticated laugh.*) – Not with a lion, of course, but exactly this sudden flash of light. . . !

LYMAN. The whole future is clear to me now! We are not going to sidle shamefully into our late middle age, we're marching in heads up! I'm going to build a selfish little cottage in the Caribbean and we'll fill it up with all the thick English novels we never got to finish . . . plus Proust! – and I'll buy two mopeds with little baskets on the handlebars for the shopping trips . . .

THEO. I knew it, I knew it!

LYMAN. . . . And I'll spend every day with you – except maybe a week or two a month in the Elmira office!

BESSIE. How fantastic, Mother!

THEO. Thank you, lion! Thank you, Africa! (*Turning to him.*) Lyman?

LYMAN (*already mentally departing the present*). . . . Huh?

Yes!

THEO. I am all new!

*She throws her arms around him, burying her face in his neck.
He looks front with an expression of deepening agony.*

BESSIE. This has been the most fantastic two weeks of my
life! I love you, Daddy!

*She rushes to him and with one arm he embraces her, the other
around* THEO; *tears starting into his eyes.*

BESSIE. Are you weeping?

LYMAN. Just amazement, honey . . . at my luck, I guess.
Come, we'd better go back.

*Sombrely he turns them upstage; lights are changing, growing
dimmer and they walk into darkness while he remains behind.
Alone − in his hospital gown still − he slowly turns front;
light spreads and reveals the* NURSE *sitting near the bed
and cast.*

NURSE (*to the cast, exactly as earlier*). The only thing I don't
understand is why you married that woman, a smart man
like you.

LYMAN *stares ahead as* LEAH *appears, isolated in light;
she is in her fur coat, exactly as in Act One when she was
about to go for an abortion. The* NURSE *remains on the
periphery, immobile.*

LEAH. Yes, I suppose it could wait a week or so, but
. . . really, Lyman, you know you're never going to
leave her.

LYMAN. You cancel the operation, okay? And I'm telling
her tomorrow.

LEAH. You're telling her what?

LYMAN (*almost holding his breath*). I will not rationalize you
away. I have one life! I'm going to ask her for a divorce.

LEAH. My God, Lyman!

LYMAN (*pulls her into his arms*). Why are we so *connected*?
− Do you feel it?

LEAH. I don't understand it. I seem to have known you forever. But listen, I know your attachment to her . . .

LYMAN. I trust you . . . I'd like to tell you something. (*He takes a pause out of sheer caution.*) I had a son once, with a terrific girl I knew. A long time ago now. – I'm ashamed of this – I convinced her to have it. I was crazy about her. But I had to break it off or lose my marriage. It was torture. – About seventeen years later I am checking into Pan Am in Los Angeles, and I see this young guy in line in front of me. My spitting image. Unmistakable. When he laid his ticket on the counter the clerk said his name, sure enough – it was his mother's. We sat facing each other in the waiting area. I was paralyzed.

LEAH. Why couldn't you have introduced yourself!

LYMAN. Well, he was dressed kind of poor . . . and he had an unhappy look. He'd have to feel I'd betrayed him, I was sure he'd hate me . . . (*Pause; he kisses her hand.*) Please keep this baby. Will you? And stay home and cross your legs, you hear? – no dates.

LEAH. But stop worrying about another man, okay? – Please, I'm not really like that, if I'm committed.

LYMAN (*with mock anger squeezes her cheeks together*). A nunnery for you till I get back, you hear?

LEAH. This is serious?

LYMAN. This is serious.

LEAH. Suddenly . . . why am I not sure I want to be a mother! – Do I, you think?

LYMAN. Yes you do, I think!

Kisses her. They laugh together. He turns to leave; she grasps his hands and presses them together between hers in a prayerful gesture; and facing heaven . . .

LEAH. Please! Some good luck! (*To him directly.*) Why is everything so dangerous!

She gives him a violent kiss. She walks into darkness and, as he turns, THEO *appears walking; she is hiding something behind her back and smiling lovingly.* LYMAN *looks solemn, prepared for the showdown.*

LYMAN. Theo, dear . . . There's something I have to tell you . . .

THEO (*holding out a cashmere sweater*). Happy birthday!

LYMAN (*startled*). Hah? But it's not July, is it!

THEO. But it was so sinfully expensive I needed an excuse. (*Putting him into the sweater.*) Here . . . straighten it. It's Italian. It's not too big, is it? (*Stepping back to admire.*) It's gorgeous, look in the mirror!

LYMAN. It's beautiful, thank you, dear. But listen, I really have something to . . .

THEO. My God, Lyman, you are simply magnificent! (*Linking arms and walking in her cumbersome way.*) I have another surprise – I got tickets for the Ballanchine! And a table at Luigi's afterwards!

LYMAN (*grimly screwing up his courage – and he is beginning to resent her domination*). I have something to tell you, Theo, why do you make it so hard for me!

THEO. What?

He is paralyzed.

What is it? Has something happened? (*Alarmed now.*) Lyman! (*Asking.*) – You went for your checkup!

LYMAN (*about to explode*). God's sake, no, it's not that!

THEO. Why is your face so grey? Please, what is it, you look terrified!

He moves away from her and her awful caring, and halts facing front. She moves off and calls to him from the distance.

– I'll ring my cousin Wilbur, he's still at Mass. General, we can go up there together. . . ! Please, darling, don't worry about anything. . . ! What is it, can you tell me?

In total blockage – both in the past and present – he inhales deeply and lets out a gigantic long howl, arms raised, imploring

*heaven for relief. In effect, it blasts her out of his mind – she
de-animates and goes dark, and he is alone again.*

LYMAN (*to himself, facing front*). No guts. That's the whole
story. No guts!

A hospital gurney rolls on. LEAH *is lying on it. She raises
up on her elbows.*

LEAH. You got here!

LYMAN (*grinning broadly*). Of course I got here!

LEAH. Have they shown him to you? He's a boy! – And
you see how he looks like you?

LYMAN. No, not me – like my father after a shave. (*Kisses
her.*) What an airy softness on your eyes; like God leaned
down and lightly kissed your breast.

LEAH. I was so hoping you'd come. (*Kisses his hand.*) Thank
you for him, darling. I love you. And I do understand why
you can't divorce her, and it's okay. Really. In fact, it's
ironical, you make me understand what real commitment
means.

LYMAN. I love you, Leah. You have a sublime gift of
nearness . . .

LEAH. You'll still come and see us, won't you? – When
you can? (*He covers his face.*) Don't feel bad, we could
still have a good life! What can I name him?

LYMAN (*lowering his hands, in the throes of loss*). I filled out
the form for you.

LEAH (*laughs*). You did?

LYMAN. I put down Benjamin, is that okay?

LEAH. If it's from you it's beautiful. What about a second
name? – I guess mine, huh?

LYMAN. I want to put down Felt. – In fact, I did.

LEAH. Felt! – How will I explain that to him?

LYMAN (*hesitates . . . then, with a tense smile . . .*) I know
you owe me nothing, darling, but they tell me there's
been a man coming in to see you.

LEAH. A doctor; he stops by; I used to know him. But
truthfully . . . I do feel more sure I'm going to end

up married. Maybe not, but definitely maybe – I mean
some day.

LYMAN. With who?

LEAH. I don't know! When I came out of the anaesthetic, I
thought – maybe if I was married we could both be guilty,
and it would make it easier for you.

LYMAN. I'm not even going to try to understand that.

LEAH (*laughing, she suddenly weeps* . . .). Please go, dear,
I can't bear this . . . Come later if you can or just write
me – or call me up and make me laugh!

LYMAN. Oh, my darling, my darling . . . we've got to stay
together!

LEAH (*angering*). But you can't! – Why do you keep saying
that!

LYMAN. What if I got you a loft downtown in the city, and
I'd buy you out here and you can stay home with him and
paint? – What do you say? I'd set up a trust fund . . .

LEAH. Why don't we just play it by ear?

LYMAN. Meaning what?

LEAH. Come up when you can, and we'll meet in the city
sometimes when I come down . . .

LYMAN. . . . My heart's going to die . . . you're drifting
away!

LEAH (*direct and tough*). . . . But how can I commit myself
and you just stop by now and then. . . . I mean sooner
or later won't that irritate me? – You poor man, you're
so divided . . . or do you think you're too old?

*Tremendously conflicted, he avoids her eyes. She strokes his
face.*

Well, don't get depressed; we are how we are. . . . Anyway,
I'm not absolutely sure I should be married to anybody –
I think I may still be too curious.

LYMAN. About men?

She nods, mystified. He is suddenly decisive.

Give me a month. By June first I either settle with Theo
or I disappear, okay?

LEAH. You poor man. I wish I could help you, but I'm so mixed up myself . . .

LYMAN. I've lost my judgement, I'm out of sync with my age and I'm being foolish.

LEAH. But you are not old, you're a sensualist and romantic, and I think it's just marvellous!

LYMAN (*he is moving into a light and she is vanishing*). No! I know what's wrong with me – I could never stand still for death! Which you've got to do, by a certain age, or be ridiculous – you've got to stand there nobly and serene . . .

LEAH is gone now, he's alone.

. . . and let death run his tape out your arms and around your belly and up your crotch until he's got you fitted for that last black suit. And I can't, I won't! . . . So I'm left wrestling with this anachronistic energy which . . .

as he enters the cast, crying out to the world . . .

. . . God has charged me with and I will use it till the dirt is shovelled into my mouth! Life! Life! Fuck death and dying!

Light widens, finding LEAH in the present, dressed differently than in the previous – in her fur coat – standing near the bed with the NURSE, listening to his shouts.

NURSE. Don't be afraid, just wait a minute, he comes out of it. I'm sure he wants to see you.

LEAH (*moving tentatively to the cast*). Lyman?

He looks at her with cloudy recognition.

It's me, Leah.

NURSE *exits.*

LYMAN (*now fully aware of her*). Leah! (*Turning away from her.*) Jesus, what have I done to you! – Wait . . . (*A moment; he looks around.*) Was Theo here?

LEAH. I think she's gone, I just got here.

LYMAN. I don't know where the hell I am. . . . Oh, Leah, it's sitting on my chest like a bag of cement.

LEAH. What is?

LYMAN. My character.

LEAH. Yes, well . . . it's pretty bad.

LYMAN. And still, I swear, all I've ever done is try to be honest. (*Moved.*) Thanks for coming.

LEAH. I only came about Benny, I don't know how to begin explaining this to him.

LYMAN (*about to weep again*). What balls you have to come here and talk so coolly, I really salute you. – What's he saying?

LEAH (*frustrated, she turns away*). He's excited that he has a sister.

LYMAN (*painful admiration*). Oh, that dear boy!

LEAH. He's very badly mixed up, Lyman; he's seen us all on TV and one of the other kids told him he has two mothers. He sweats in his sleep. He keeps asking me are you coming home again. It's twisting my heart. I'm terrified if this isn't settled right it could screw up the rest of his life. (*Tears start.*) You're his idol, Lyman! – His god!

LYMAN. Oh, the wreckage, the wreckage . . .

LEAH. Tell me the truth; it's okay if you don't, I just want to know – do you feel a responsibility or not?

LYMAN (*flaring up, scared as much as indignant*). How can you ask such a thing?

LEAH. Why! That's a reasonable question!

LYMAN. Now you listen – I know I'm wrong and I'm wrong and I'm wrong but I did not throw you both across my saddle to rape you in my tent! You knew I was married, and you tried to make me love you, so I'm not entirely . . .

LEAH. Lyman, if you're blaming me I'm going to sink through this floor!

LYMAN. I'm talking about truth not blame – this is not entirely a one-man disaster!

LEAH. It's amazing, the minute you talk about truth you always come out looking better than anybody else!

LYMAN. Now that's unfair!

LEAH (*slight pause*). I want to talk about Benny.

LYMAN. You could bring him tomorrow if you like. But go ahead, we can talk now.

A pause as she settles down.

LEAH (*a flushed grin*). Incidentally . . . I'm just curious, how's everything with your wife? – They tell me you spent over an hour with her.

LYMAN. All she did was sit there telling me I'm a monster who never loved anybody.

LEAH (*with a hard grin*). And I suppose you reassured her otherwise.

LYMAN. Well, I did love her. Just as I loved you. The truth is the truth, kid.

LEAH. What a piece of work you are, Lyman, really – you go falling off a mountain and you still don't understand anything.

LYMAN. What should I understand?

LEAH. Never mind.

LYMAN. Well what?

LEAH (*anxiety and anger*). It's no business of mine, but your hatred for that woman is monumental. I mean it's . . . *oceanic*.

LYMAN. What the hell are you going on about!

LEAH. Because it's unnerving to have to listen to this shit all over again!

LYMAN. What shit? What have I said!

LEAH. My dear man, in case it slipped your mind, when I was two months pregnant we went to New York and you picked the Carlyle Hotel to stay at – four blocks from your house! 'Loved her' – good G. . . !

A window begins to appear upstage with THEO *seated in profile, reading a book. He is staring as he emerges from the cast, turning to look up at the window . . .* LEAH *goes on with no pause.*

What was all that about if it wasn't hatred! – And walking me past your front window with her sitting there. . . ? And – yes, my God I almost forgot – going in to see her yet? You had murder in you and you still do! – probably for me too!

LYMAN (*glancing up at* THEO *in the window*). But it didn't feel like murder at all. I was dancing the high wire on the edge of the world . . . finally risking everything to find myself! – Strolling with you past my house, the spring breeze, the lingerie in the Madison Avenue shop windows, the swish of . . . wasn't it a taffeta skirt you wore? . . . and my new baby coiled in your belly? – I'd beaten guilt forever!

She is moving toward him, part of his recall.

. . . And how languorous you were, your pregnant glory bulging under the streetlamp!

She takes on the ease of that long-ago stroll, and. . . .

LEAH. Is that her?

LYMAN *looks up at* THEO *then at* LEAH, *inspired, alive.*

LYMAN. Oh, Leah darling, how sexy you look against tall buildings.

LEAH (*warm smile, taking his arm*). You're tense, aren't you?

LYMAN. Well, I've lived here with her for so many years . . .

LEAH. Was she very upset when you told her?

LYMAN (*tragically; but hesitates*). . . . Yes, dear, she was.

LEAH. Well, maybe she'll marry again in time.

LYMAN (*a glance to the window; he loosens her grip on his arm*). I doubt it, somehow.

LEAH (*an intrigued smile*). Mustn't we touch?

LYMAN (*quickly regaining her arm*). Of course!

They start walking away.

LEAH. I'd love to meet her some time . . . just as friends.

LYMAN. You might.

LEAH. You're still feeling guilty, aren't you?

LYMAN (*halts; a strange determination suddenly*). A little, yes. And I hate it. – Listen, I'd like to see if I can go in and say hello.

LEAH. Really? Would you like me to come?

LYMAN. Not just yet. Would you mind a lot? Tell me.

LEAH. No, go ahead. I kind of like it that you don't just drop people.

LYMAN. God, you have balls! I'll see you back at the hotel in twenty minutes, okay?

LEAH. Take your time! I'll play with all that gorgeous underwear you bought. (*Touching her belly.*) I'm so contented, Lyman!

She turns and walks away. He remains below the window, staring at her departing figure.

LYMAN. Why is it, the happier she is the sadder I get? It's this damned *objectivity*! – Like God must feel when he looks at happy people – knowing what he knows about worms! (*Now he looks up at* THEO, *and his heart sinks.*) What have I done! Have I only doubled the distance that I stand from my life? (*Violent determination.*) Idiot! – love her! Now that she doesn't deprive you any more let love flow to your wise and wonderful wife! To hell with this guilt!

He rushes toward THEO, *but then turns away in terror, walking around in a circle and blowing out air and covering his face. Now gritting his teeth he again hurries toward the window . . . which disappears, as she rises, startled.*

THEO. Lyman! – you said Tuesday, didn't you?

He takes her in his arms, kisses her with frantic passion. She is surprised and happy.

LYMAN. What a handsome lady! Theo, you are God's handwriting.

LEAH. Ralph Waldo Emerson.

LYMAN. Some day I'm going to swipe an image you never heard of!

Laughing, in comradely style, embraces her closely as he takes her to a seat – turning on a certain excited intimacy here.

Listen, I hitched a ride down with this pilot in his new Cessna – I have meetings up there starting seven-thirty tomorrow but I just had to astonish you.

LEAH. You flew in a small plane *at night*?

LYMAN. That whole fear was guilt, Theo – I thought I *deserved* to crash. But I deserve to live because I am not a bad guy and I love you.

THEO. Well, I'm floating away! When must you go back?

LYMAN. Now.

THEO (*near laughter at the absurdity*). Can't we even chat?

LYMAN. No. In fact, I'd better call that I'm on my way.

Goes to a point, mimes 'dialling'.

THEO. I'll drive you to the airport.

LYMAN. He's picking me up at the Carlyle . . . Hello?

LEAH *lights, holding a mimed phone.*

LEAH. Darling!

LYMAN. Be there in ten minutes.

LEAH (*puzzled*). Oh? Okay. Why are you calling?

LYMAN. Just to be sure you didn't forget me and took off.

LEAH (*a laugh at his charm*). Your jealousy is so comforting! – You know, she made a very dignified picture, reading in the window – it was like an Edward Hopper, kind of haunted.

LYMAN. Yes. Well, I'm leaving right now. (*Mimes hanging up.*)

THEO. You won't forget about dinner Thursday with Leona and Gilbert . . . he's gotten his hearing aid so it won't be so bad.

LYMAN (*with a certain solemnity, taking her hands*). – I just

had to steal this extra look at one another . . . life's so
stupidly short, Theo.

THEO (*happily*). Why is Death always over your shoulder?
You've got more life in you than anybody! (*Ruffling his
hair.*) In fact, you're kind of sparkly tonight.

LYMAN (*breathlessly*). – Listen, we have time to make love.

THEO (*a surprised, delighted laugh*). I wish I knew what's
come over you!

LYMAN. That I'm alive, that's all! – I've got to have you!
(*He starts to lead her.*) I keep forgetting what a sweet piece
of ass my wife is!

THEO. Must be the new office in Elmira – beginnings are
always exciting!

LYMAN (*turning her to him he kisses her mouth, feeling her
body*). I keep meaning to ask you – has there ever been
a god who was guilty?

THEO. Gods are never guilty, that's why they're gods –
except Jesus, of course.

LYMAN (*kisses her reverently*). I feel like the moon's in my
belly and the sun's in my mouth and I'm shining down
on the world. (*Laughs with a self-mocking charm.*) . . . A
regular planetary flashlight! Come!

*And laughing in high tension takes her hand and moves her
into darkness . . .*

THEO. Oh, Lyman – how wonderfully, endlessly changing
you are!

Blackout.

Light up on LEAH *in hospital room;* LYMAN *is back in
his cast.*

LEAH. So you bopped her that night.

LYMAN. What can I say?

LEAH. There's just no end to you, is there? – And when
you came back to the hotel, didn't we . . . ?

LYMAN. I couldn't keep myself, I was exploding with life!

Maybe it was that you were so close by, waiting for me, but she seemed absolutely gorgeous! How can that be evil?

LEAH (*a sigh*). – Listen, I have to talk business. I want the house transferred to my name immediately.

LYMAN. What are you saying? Leah . . . !

LEAH. I know how much feeling you put into it but I want the security for Benny's sake.

LYMAN. Leah, I beg you to wait with that . . .

LEAH. I will not wait with that!! And I want my business returned to me.

LYMAN. That'll be complicated – it's many times bigger than when I took it over . . .

LEAH. I want it back!! I would have expanded without you! I'm not going to be a *total* fool! I will sue you!

LYMAN. Okay, okay. Done.

LEAH (*opening her pocket book*). I don't think you'll want to get into a court just now . . .

LYMAN (*a very uncertain grin*). You'd really sue me?

LEAH (*searching in her pocketbook*). I'm not fooling around, Lyman. You've hurt me very deeply . . . (*Breaks off, holding back tears. She takes out a sheet of paper.*)

LYMAN (*forced to turn from her*). Jesus, how I hate to see you cry.

LEAH. I have something I want you to sign.

LYMAN. To *sign*?

LEAH. It's a quit-claim on the house and my business. Will you read it?

LYMAN. You're not serious.

LEAH. I had Ted Lester draw it up. Here, read it.

LYMAN. I know what a quit-claim is, don't tell me to read a quit-claim. How can you do this?

LEAH. We aren't married and I don't want you making claims on me.

LYMAN. And . . . and what about Benny. You don't mean you're taking Benny from me . . .

LEAH. I . . .

LYMAN. I want you to bring him here tomorrow morning so I can talk to him.

LEAH. Just a minute . . .

LYMAN. Now you're going to bring him, Leah . . .

LEAH. You listen to me! I've been through this with Ted Lester and you haven't a legal leg to stand on. I will not allow you to see him until I know what you intend to say to him about all this.

LYMAN. I'll tell him the truth – I love him.

LEAH. You love him.

LYMAN (*threateningly*). I said I love him, Leah!

LEAH. But what is he going to make of that? – That it's all right to deceive people you love?

LYMAN. Human beings can lose control when they fall in love, it won't hurt him to know that. You're over-protecting him.

LEAH. But how is he going to figure this out? – You love him and lied to him so terribly? – He's all I have now, Lyman, I am not going to see him go crazy!

LYMAN. Now you stop that! I did a helluva lot more than lie to him . . .

LEAH (*outpouring*). You lied to him! – Why don't you seem to register this? The whole thing was a lie!

LYMAN. I love that boy!

LEAH. . . . To buy him the pony, and teach him to ski, and take him up in the glider . . . you made him worship you – when you knew what you knew! That was cruelty!

LYMAN. All right, I won't argue. What do you think I should tell him?

LEAH. I think you have to say that you do love him but he mustn't follow your example because lying to people injures them. And you beg his pardon, and promise you'll never mislead him again.

LYMAN. I am not grinding myself up in front of my son's face! That is not education for him, kid, it's your revenge on me! And if I can teach him anything now it's to have the guts to be true to himself! That's all that matters!

LEAH. Even if he has to betray the whole world to do it?

LYMAN (*in an agony*). Only the truth is sacred, Leah! – To hold back nothing!

LEAH. You must be crazy – you held back everything! – You really don't know right from wrong, do you!

LYMAN. Jesus Christ, you sound like Theo!

LEAH. Well maybe it's what happens to people who marry you! Look – I don't think it's a good idea at the moment . . .

LYMAN. I have a right to see my son!

LEAH. I won't have him copying you, Lyman, it will destroy his life! (*She starts to leave.*)

LYMAN. I want Benny! I want Benny, Leah! You will bring me Benny!

Enter BESSIE *alone. She is extremely tense and anxious.*

BESSIE. Oh! I'm so glad you're still here. Listen . . .

LEAH. I was just going . . .

BESSIE. Please don't! She's had an attack of some kind – they're looking at her in a room down the hall.

LYMAN. My God, Bessie . . . what is it?

BESSIE. I really think it would help if she saw that you're together . . .

LEAH. But we're not together.

BESSIE. Oh! – Well, I'm not too sorry to hear that, I thought you were going to let him get away with it.

LYMAN. Well it isn't quite settled . . .

LEAH. Maybe it is, dear. (*To* BESSIE.) – What did you mean? – to see we're together?

BESSIE. – She talks about taking him home with her.

LYMAN. No kidding!

BESSIE (*a quick hostile glance at him, then . . .*). She's a little delusionary.

LEAH. Oh how awful!

BESSIE. . . . I wonder . . . if you could talk to her and tell her your feelings, maybe it would get her back to some reality about him.

LEAH. I'm sorry, dear, but I'm at the outer edge of my nervous system, I just couldn't start to . . .

LYMAN. Why must it be a delusion? Maybe Mother really wants me back . . .

BESSIE (*a frustrated stamp of her foot*). I want her out of here and home!

LYMAN. What should I do, stick horns on my head and a tail on my ass? I am not a monster, Bessie! My God, where did all this cruelty come from!

LEAH. He wants her, you see . . .

LYMAN. I want you both!

BESSIE (*with a hysterical overtone, screaming*). Will you once in your life think of another human being?

TOM and THEO enter with the NURSE; he has her by the arm. She has a heightened, 'seeing' air about her, a fixed dead smile and her head trembles.

LYMAN. Theo! – come, sit her down, Tom!

LEAH (*to BESSIE; fearfully*). I really feel I ought to go . . .

THEO. Oh, I wish you could stay a few minutes! (*To NURSE.*) Please get a chair for Mrs Felt.

The reference causes surprise in BESSIE. LEAH looks quickly to BESSIE, perplexed because this is the opposite of what she said THEO wished. LYMAN is immensely encouraged by it. The NURSE, as she goes out for the chair, glances about, perplexed.

THEO. Well! Here we are all together.

Slight pause.

TOM. She's had a little . . . incident, Lyman. (*To BESSIE.*) I've arranged for a plane; the three of us can go to the city together.

BESSIE. Oh, good. – We're ready to leave whenever you say, Mother.

LYMAN. Thanks, Theo . . . for coming.

THEO (*turns to him, smiling blankly*). Socialism is dead. (*A beat.*) And Christianity is finished, so . . . (*Searches.*) There is really nothing left to . . . to . . . Except simplicity? To defend? (*She crosses her legs, and her coat falls partially open revealing a bare thigh.*)

BESSIE. Mother! – where's your skirt?

THEO. I'm comfortable, it's all right . . .

NURSE *enters with a chair.*

BESSIE. She must have left her skirt in the room she was just in – would you get it, please?

NURSE, *perplexed again, exits.*

THEO (*to* LEAH). I wish I hadn't carried on that way . . . I'm sorry. (*Turning to* LYMAN.) The surprise is what threw me. I was just totally unprepared. But I'm better now. (*To* LEAH.) I'm really much better. (*Breaks off.*) Do you see the *Village Voice* up here?

LEAH. Yes, occasionally.

THEO. There was a strange interview some years back with Isaac Bashevis Singer, the novelist? The interviewer was a woman whose husband had left her for another woman and she couldn't understand why. And Singer said, 'Maybe he liked her hole better'. I was shocked at the time, really outraged – you know, that he'd gotten a Nobel; but now I think it was courageous to have said that, because it's probably true. Courage . . . courage is always the main thing! Everyone knows that, of course, but suddenly it is so . . . so *clear* . . .

NURSE *enters, offers her the skirt.*

NURSE. Can I help you on with it?

THEO (*takes the skirt, looks at it without recognition and drops it on the floor*). I can't remember if I called you Leah or Mrs Felt.

LEAH. I'm not really Mrs Felt.

THEO (*a pleasant social smile*). Well, it doesn't really matter – I guess we're all sort of interchangeable anyway. Except for the children. (*Short pause.*) Your boy needs his father, I imagine.

LEAH. Well . . . yes, but . . .

THEO. Then he should be here with you, shouldn't he? (*To* LYMAN.) You can come up here whenever you want to . . . if that's what you'd like to do.

BESSIE (*to* TOM). She's really too ill for this. – Come, Mother, we're going . . .

THEO (*to* LYMAN). I can say 'fuck', you know. I never cared for the word but I'm sure she has her limitations too. I can say 'fuck me', 'fuck you'; whatever.

LYMAN *is silent in guilty anguish.*

BESSIE (*to* LYMAN, *furiously*). Will you tell her to leave? – Just out of respect, out of friendship!

LYMAN. Yes. (*Delicately.*) She's right, Theo, I think that would be the best . . .

THEO (*to* BESSIE). No, I can take better care of him at home. (*To* LEAH.) I really have nothing to do, and you're busy, I imagine . . .

BESSIE. Tom, will you . . . ?

TOM. Why don't we let her say what's on her mind?

THEO (*to* BESSIE). He had every right to resent me. What did I ever do but correct him? (*To* LEAH.) You don't correct him, do you. You like him as he is, even now, don't you. And that's the secret, isn't it. (*To* LYMAN.) Well I can do that. I don't need to correct you . . . or rather pretend to . . .

BESSIE. I can't bear this, Mother!

THEO (*calmly to* BESSIE). But Bessie dear, I've always pretty well known what he was doing. I think I have, anyway; why have I tolerated it? (*Suddenly screams at the top of her lungs.*) Why have I tolerated it!

Silence. Fear in all of them.

BESSIE (*terrified for her mother*). Daddy, please . . . tell her . . . ?

LYMAN. But she's trying to tell the truth, darling.

LEAH (*suddenly filling up*). You poor woman! (*To him.*) – What a bastard you are; one honest sentence from you and none of this would have happened, it's despicable! (*Appealing to* THEO.) I'm so sorry about it, Mrs Felt . . .

THEO. No-no . . . he's absolutely right – he's always said

it – it's life I can't bear! But you accept it, you trust it, and that's why you *should* win out . . .

LEAH. But it's not true – I never really trusted him! Not really! Not really *trusted*. To tell you the truth, I never wanted to marry anybody, I've never known one happy couple! – Listen, you mustn't blame yourself, the whole damned thing doesn't work, it never works . . . which I knew and went ahead and did it anyway and I'll never understand why!

LYMAN (*bitter anger*). Because if you hadn't married me you wouldn't have kept Benny. Don't start being a dumb-bell, Leah!

She can't find words.

– You wouldn't have had Benny or this last nine years of your happiness. You've become the woman you always wanted to be, instead of . . . (*Catches himself.*) Well, what's the difference?

LEAH. No, don't stop – instead of what? What did you save me from?

LYMAN (*accepting her challenge*). All right . . . from all those lonely post-coital showerbaths, and the pointless pillow talk and the boxes of heartless condoms beside your bed . . .

LEAH (*speechless*). Well now!

LYMAN. I'm sick of this crap, Leah! – You got a little something out of this despicable treachery!

THEO. That's a terrible thing to say to the woman.

LYMAN. But the truth is terrible, isn't that what you've just finished saying? Are you still looking for your purity, Theo? You tolerated me because you loved me, and more than I deserved, but wasn't it also the good life I gave you. – Well, what's wrong with that? Aren't women people? Don't people love power? I don't understand the disgrace!

BESSIE (*to both women*). Why are you still sitting here, don't you have any pride! – (*To* LEAH.) This is disgusting!

LEAH. Will you please stop challenging everybody? I have

business with him, so I have to talk to him! – I'll go out of my mind here! Am I being accused of something?

BESSIE. You shouldn't be in the same room with him!

LEAH (*rattled*). I just explained that, didn't I? *What the hell do you want!*

LYMAN (*through a cry*). She wants her father back!

BESSIE. You son of a bitch! (*Raises her fists, then weeps helplessly.*)

LYMAN. I love you, Bessie! – All of you! You are all magnificent!

BESSIE. You ought to be killed!

She bursts into tears. A helpless river of grief which now overflows to sweep up LYMAN; *then* LEAH *is carried away by the wave of weeping. All strategies collapse as finally* THEO *is infected. The four of them are helplessly covering their faces. It is a veritable mass keening, a funerary explosion of grief, each for his or her own condition, for love's frustration and for the end of all their capacity to reason.*

TOM *has turned from them, head bent in prayer, hands clasped, eyes shut.*

LYMAN. Theo, please! – Put some clothes on! (*Turning for help to* TOM.) Tom, I can't bear her doing this. . . ! (*Breaks off.*) Are you praying, for Christ's sake?

TOM (*staring ahead, only glancing at them*). There is no way to go forward. You must all stop loving him. You must, or he will destroy you. He is an endless string attached to nothing. – Theo needs help now, Lyman, and I don't want a conflict, so I don't see how I can go on representing you.

LYMAN. – Why? Am I not worthy? Who is not an endless string? (*A shout, but with the strain of his loss, his inability to connect.*) Who is attached to something in this world now? – I am human, I am proud of it! – Of the glory and the shit!

TOM. You must face it, Lyman, you moved that barrier . . .

LYMAN. That was not suicide – I am not a cop-out!

TOM. Why is it a cop-out to have a conscience? You were ashamed, weren't you? Why can't you acknowledge that? Isn't a conscience human? Your shame is the best part of you, for God's sake . . . ! (*Breaks off, giving it up.*) – I'm ready to go, Theo.

LYMAN. Let her stay a while. (*To* THEO.) You want to stay, don't you?

BESSIE. Mother? (*She raises* THEO *to her feet. Her head is trembling. She turns to* LYMAN.)

LYMAN. You can't really leave me, Theo – you can't!

THEO. I'm afraid I have nothing . . . in me any more, Lyman.

BESSIE *takes her by the arm to go.* LEAH *stands, as though to leave.*

LYMAN. – Bessie? I'll see you again, won't I? – Some time?

BESSIE *is silent.*

Leah? – You can stay a little, can't you?

LEAH (*an evasive colour*). I have work in the office . . .

LYMAN (*with a scared laugh*). You all pulling out? – What is this?

LEAH. I'll try to stop by tomorrow, if I can . . .

LYMAN (*open terror at her cool tone*). I want you to bring Benny.

LEAH. . . . I can't, it's a school day . . .

LYMAN (*terrified*). You're not taking Benny from me?

She can't answer.

You bring Benny to me, Leah!

FATHER *appears, shaking out his black shroud. They are all moving to leave.*

LEAH. Stop shouting! – I can't bring him!

FATHER *flaps out the shroud which billows out before him.* LYMAN's *fear rises.*

LYMAN. Don't leave me like this, for Christ's sake! (*They continue moving; he is terrified.*) I said wait a minute . . . ! Don't leave me, Leah, Bessie . . . Theo, listen . . . !

With a sudden billowing movement, FATHER *sweeps the black cloth billowing out over* LYMAN *on the bed, covering him completely. He shouts from underneath . . .*

No! Don't! Pa! Please! Don't do it!

LEAH. Stop this! Why are you yelling!

LYMAN (*thrashing around in terror*). Where's the light! Where is the fucking light!

LEAH (*to* TOM *for help*). What is he doing?

LYMAN *flings off the shroud, still terrified – all they see is that he has been thrashing about; and he lies there now panting for breath as* FATHER *walks into darkness trailing the shroud, muttering.*

LEAH (*starts away swiftly*). I can't bear it any more!

LYMAN (*a look of amazement*). Wait! Wait, please . . . I remember what happened! – How I got on the mountain! (*As memory floods back.*) – I kept calling you from the Howard Johnson's – yes. To tell you I'd be staying over because of the storm . . . but the line was busy. So I went to bed, yes . . . But it was still busy . . . over an hour . . . more! And I . . . yes, I started to ask the operator to cut in as an emergency, but . . . (*Breaks off.*) I remembered something you once said to me . . .

LEAH. I was talking to . . .

LYMAN (*quick fury*). I'm telling you what *happened*! – Let me finish!

LEAH. I was talking to my brother!

LYMAN. In Japan, for over an hour?

LEAH. He just got back on Monday.

LYMAN. Well, it doesn't matter.

LEAH. It certainly does matter!

LYMAN. Leah, remember you once said . . . 'I might lie to you,' remember that? Way at the beginning? It seemed so wonderful then . . . that you could be so honest; but now, on my back in that room, I started to die.

LEAH (*outraged*). I said it was my brother!

LYMAN. You're not understanding me, I'm not blaming you. I got dressed and back in the car to . . . *feel something again.* 'Cause it had all died in me, Leah – this whole ten-year commute was just . . . ludicrous! I was a corpse buried in that room; I couldn't wait . . . (*A laugh at himself.*) I know it was crazy but I thought if I walked in two-three in the morning out of a roaring blizzard like that . . . you'd be so amazed, you'd believe how I needed you . . . *and I would believe it too!* (*Near weeping.*) And maybe we'd really fall in love again.

LEAH (*covering her face, weeping*). Oh God, Lyman . . . !

He looks at them standing there in their desolation.

LYMAN. I got back in the car to stop the dying. So I know the suffering I've been for you, I tried not to but I do see it now.

Looks from one to the other; there is no agreement from them.

Then all I am is shit? Is that the last word?

But no one answers or moves.

. . . I don't understand it, do I?

No one moves.

(*Outcry.*) Help me, Bessie, what is it? What should I understand!

BESSIE. There are other people.

A long pause.

LYMAN (*staring ahead*). Yes. That's as simple as an arrow, darling. (*With a soberly wondrous acceptance.*) Okay. (*Pause.*) But I have known what love feels like, darling; for you I could give my life without a second thought. – But probably not for anybody else, so I know what

you're trying to tell me, dear girl. (*He looks at them all.*)
It's okay – if you want to go now. It's over.

BESSIE *turns away to shield her feelings.*

But I have to say this – in some miserable dark corner of
my soul I'm still not sure why I'm condemned.

They don't move; he goes perfectly still. And now with dread.

Are you hearing me? Are you in this room!

BESSIE. Come, Mother.

She smooths THEO*'s hair – her head is in noticeable tremor.*

THEO. . . . Say goodbye to him, dear.
BESSIE (*dry-eyed now; her feeling clearer, she has a close
to impersonal sound*). I hope you're better soon, Daddy.
Goodbye.

She takes her mother's arm – THEO *no longer resists as they
move out into darkness. He turns to* LEAH.

LYMAN. Oh Leah, say something tough and honest . . .
the way you can.
LEAH. I don't know if I'll ever believe anything . . . or
anybody, again.
LYMAN. Oh no. No! – I haven't done that!

A great weeping sweeps her and she rushes out.

LYMAN. Leah! *Leah!*

But she is gone.

TOM. Talk to you soon.

He sees that LYMAN *is lost in space, and he goes out. The*
NURSE *comes from her corner to him.*

NURSE. You got pain?

He doesn't reply.

I'll get you something to smooth you out.

LYMAN. Don't leave me alone, okay? – For a little while? Please. Sit with me. (*Pats the mattress.*) Come, don't be afraid.

She approaches the bed reluctantly; he draws her down to sit beside him. He takes her hand.

It's just two worlds, see? – Women want it safe, but it's dangerous. Just is. Can't help it. It's terrible. And it's okay.

NURSE (*not giving agreement*). Let me get you something. (*Starts to withdraw her hand.*)

LYMAN (*holding onto her hand*). Ten more seconds – I love your warmth, Hogan. A woman's warmth is the last sacredness; you're a piece of the sun. The last magic. – Which reminds me . . . When you're out there fishing on the ice with your husband and your boy . . . what do you talk about?

NURSE. . . . Well, let's see . . . this last time we all bought us some shoes at that big Knapp Shoe Outlet up there? – They're seconds, but you can't tell them from new.

LYMAN. So you talked about your new shoes?

NURSE. Well they're great buys.

LYMAN. Right. That . . . that's just wonderful to do that. I don't know why, but it just is.

NURSE. I'll be right back.

She starts away.

LYMAN. Hate me?

NURSE (*an embarrassed shrug*). I don't know. I got to think about it.

LYMAN. Come right back, huh? I'm still a little . . . shaky.

She leans down and kisses his forehead.

Why'd you do that?

NURSE. No reason.

She exits.

LYMAN (*painful wonder and longing in his face, his eyes wide, alive . . .*). What a miracle everything is! Absolutely everything! . . . Imagine . . . three of them sitting out there together on that lake, talking about their shoes!

He begins to weep.

Blackout.